Merry Christmas from Kentucky

by

Michelle Stone

McClanahan
Publishing House

International Standard Book Number 0-913383 56 2
Library of Congress Catalog Card Number 97 74550

Cover design and book layout by James Asher Graphics

Manufactured in the United States of America

All book order correspondence should be addressed to:

McClanahan Publishing House, Inc.
P. O. Box 100
Kuttawa, KY 42055
(502) 388-9388
1-800-544-6959

Table of Contents

Appetizers

Sausage and Broccoli Party Squares

1 package refrigerated crescent rolls
⅔ cup finely chopped, fully cooked smoked turkey sausage
2 teaspoons brown mustard
⅔ cup finely chopped broccoli
⅓ cup chopped red or green pepper
¼ cup chopped onion
¾ cup shredded cheddar cheese

Unroll crescent rolls. Pat dough onto bottom of a 9x9x2-inch baking pan, overlapping and pressing to fit. Set aside. Combine the sausage and brown mustard. Spoon evenly over dough in pan. Sprinkle with chopped broccoli, pepper, onion and cheese. Bake in a 375 degree oven about 20 minutes or until golden. Cool. Cut into 25 squares.

Mushroom and Cheese Triangles

1 cup chopped fresh mushrooms
3 ounces cream cheese, softened
¼ cup finely chopped red or green pepper
1 teaspoon white wine Worcestershire sauce
⅛ teaspoon garlic powder
12 sheets phyllo dough, thawed
⅓ cup margarine or butter, melted

Filling: Combine the mushrooms, cream cheese, pepper, Worcestershire sauce and garlic powder.

Unfold phyllo dough. Place one sheet of dough on a waxed-paper-lined surface Lightly brush with melted margarine. Place another sheet on top; brush with margarine. Cut buttered stack of phyllo lengthwise into six strips. For each triangle, spoon a slightly rounded teaspoon of the filling about 1-inch from one end of each strip. Fold the end over the filling at a 45-degree angle. Continue folding loosely to form a triangle that encloses the filling, but allows room for filling to expand. Repeat with remaining phyllo, margarine and filling to make 36 triangles. Place triangles on an ungreased baking sheet. Brush with any remaining margarine. Bake in a 375 degree oven about 18 minutes or until golden. Serve warm.

Office Party Pepperoni Bites

1 cup shredded mozzarella cheese
½ cup pepperoni
½ cup pizza sauce
20 biscuits
1 tablespoon milk
¼ cup grated Parmesan cheese

Combine mozzarella, pepperoni and pizza sauce. Set aside.

Separate biscuits. Flatten biscuits to 3-inch circles. Place 1 tablespoon of pepperoni mixture in center of each biscuit. Fold edges in and pinch edge to seal. Place seam side down on greased baking sheets. Brush with milk; sprinkle with Parmesan cheese. Bake in a 350 degree oven for 12 to 15 minutes or until golden brown. Serve warm.

Traditional Cheese Ball

2 cups shredded sharp cheddar cheese
8 ounces cream cheese
2 tablespoons margarine or butter
⅓ cup chutney, finely chopped
1 teaspoon Worcestershire sauce
Dash of hot pepper sauce
½ cup finely chopped toasted pecans or peanuts

Bring the cheese, cream cheese and margarine to room temperature. Beat cheddar cheese and margarine with an electric mixer until combined. Add cream cheese, chutney, Worcestershire sauce and hot pepper sauce. Beat until thoroughly combined. Cover and refrigerate for 3 to 24 hours. Shape the chilled cheese mixture into 1 large ball or 2 small balls. Then roll the ball(s) in the nuts. Serve with crackers. Makes 1 large or 2 small cheese balls.

Christmas Party Meatballs

10 ounces cheddar cheese
1 pound sausage
2½ cups biscuit mix
1 teaspoon garlic powder
1 heaping teaspoon parsley flakes

Preheat oven to 350 degrees. Cut cheese into cubes; place in top of double boiler. Cook over hot water, stirring frequently until melted. Mix sausage, biscuit mix, garlic and parsley in large bowl. Add cheese and mix well. Shape into dime size balls. Place on a cookie sheet and bake for 15 minutes.

Holiday Meatballs

1 beaten egg
¼ cup fine dry bread crumbs
2 tablespoons snipped fresh cilantro or parsley
2 cloves garlic, minced
⅛ teaspoon ground red pepper
1 pound lean ground beef
¼ cup finely chopped peanuts
20 ounces pineapple chunks, drained
8 ounces maraschino cherries
Sweet-Sour Sauce

Combine egg, bread crumbs, cilantro, garlic, salt and pepper. Add beef and peanuts; mix well. Shape into 1-inch meatballs. Place in a 15x10x1-inch shallow baking pan. Bake in a 350 degree oven for 20 minutes or until no longer pink. Remove from oven. Drain. Thread a pineapple chunk, cherry and a meatball on a wooden toothpick. Return to baking pan. Repeat with remaining fruit and the meatballs. Brush with Sweet-Sour Sauce. Bake 5 to 8 minutes more or until heated through. In a small saucepan, heat remaining sauce until bubbly. Brush meatballs and fruit with sauce before serving. Makes 36 appetizers.

Sweet-Sour Sauce

½ cup packed brown sugar
4 teaspoons cornstarch
½ cup chicken broth
⅓ cup red wine vinegar
2 tablespoons corn syrup
2 tablespoons soy sauce
1 clove garlic, minced
2 teaspoons grated gingerroot

In a small saucepan stir together brown sugar and cornstarch. Stir in chicken broth, vinegar, corn syrup, soy sauce, garlic and gingerroot. Cook and stir until thickened and bubbly. Cook 2 minutes more. Makes about 1¼ cups.

Celebration Spinach Dip

20 ounces frozen chopped spinach, thawed and well drained
8 ounces cream cheese, cut up
2 tablespoons milk
2 cloves garlic, minced
¼ teaspoon finely shredded lemon peel
1 tablespoon lemon juice
2 teaspoons Worcestershire sauce
¼ teaspoon salt
¼ teaspoon hot pepper sauce
¼ cup sliced green onion

Combine the spinach, cream cheese, milk, garlic, lemon peel, lemon juice, Worcestershire sauce, salt and hot pepper sauce. Beat with an electric mixer on medium speed until combined. Stir in the sliced onion. Cover and chill until ready to serve.

Holiday Spicy Cheese Spread

8 ounces cream cheese, softened
1 tablespoon milk
1 clove garlic, crushed
½ teaspoon dried oregano
½ teaspoon chili powder
⅛ teaspoon ground cumin
Paprika

Combine first 6 ingredients; spoon into ½-cup containers and sprinkle with paprika. Cover and chill at least 8 hours.

Angel's Wings

2 cans refrigerated crescent rolls
2 tablespoons poppy seeds
2 tablespoons sesame seeds

Open 1 can of rolls and separate into 2 long rectangles. Press perforations to seal. Using a knife, cut rectangles in half crosswise, forming 4 small rectangles. Cut each rectangle in half, forming 8 squares. Cut each square diagonally to form 4 triangles. Repeat procedure with other can of rolls.

Press 3 triangles together on a baking sheet to resemble an angel body and wings. Roll 1 triangle into a ball; dip into poppy seeds to resemble hair. Press ball against body and wings to resemble head. Sprinkle wings with sesame seeds. Repeat procedure on remaining triangles. Bake at 375 degrees for 5 minutes or until rolls are golden. With a spatula carefully transfer to a serving plate. Makes 16 angels.

Cherry Tomatoes with Crabmeat

36 cherry tomatoes
Salt
¼ cup cottage cheese
1½ teaspoons minced onion
1½ teaspoons lemon juice
½ teaspoon horseradish
Dash of garlic salt
½ pound crabmeat, drained and flaked
¼ cup minced celery
1 tablespoon finely chopped green pepper

Cut top off each tomato; scoop out pulp. Sprinkle inside of tomato with salt and invert on paper towels to drain. Blend cottage cheese until smooth. Add next 4 ingredients, blending well. Stir in remaining ingredients. Spoon crabmeat mixture into tomatoes. Chill before serving. Makes 36 appetizers.

Vegetables Vinaigrette

1 bunch broccoli, cut into bite size pieces, discarding lower stalks
1 head cauliflower, broken into flowerets
1 pound brussels sprouts
¾ pound baby carrots, scraped
½ pound mushrooms
1 pint cherry tomatoes
1 large cucumber, sliced
2 cups water
1 cup white wine vinegar
2 teaspoons sugar
1 teaspoon dry mustard
1 teaspoon paprika
1 teaspoon dried whole oregano
¼ teaspoon dried whole thyme
4 cloves garlic, crushed

Steam broccoli, cauliflower, brussels sprouts and carrots separately until crisp-tender; drain well and chill. Place mushrooms, tomatoes, cucumber and steamed vegetables in a glass or plastic container. Combine remaining ingredients in a jar; cover tightly and shake vigorously. Pour over vegetables; cover and refrigerate overnight. Drain vegetables and arrange on a serving platter. Makes 20 servings.

Sugared Fruit Treat

Assorted whole fruit:
(grapes, pears, apples, plums, peaches, apricots, cherries, nectarines)
2 teaspoons meringue powder
4 tablespoons water
Granulated sugar

Wash all fruit. Allow fruit to dry on paper towels. In a custard cup combine the meringue powder and water. Stir with a wire whisk or fork until the powder is completely dissolved. Place sugar in a shallow plate. Dip small fruit into liquid and roll in sugar. Brush liquid onto larger fruit and spoon sugar over. Allow fruit to dry before stacking.

Beer-Cheese Spread

2 cups shredded cheddar cheese
3 ounces cream cheese, softened
2 tablespoons minced fresh parsley
1 clove garlic, crushed
⅛ teaspoon salt
¼ teaspoon hot pepper sauce
⅓ cup beer

Mix all ingredients, mixing only enough beer to give a good spreading consistency. Cover and chill several hours. For easier spreading, remove from refrigerator half hour before serving. Use as a spread on assorted breads and crackers. Makes 1½ cups.

Carol Asher
Especially Herbs

Beverages

Santa's Treat Cocoa Mix

10 cups nonfat dry milk powder
16 ounces sifted powdered sugar
1¾ cups unsweetened cocoa powder
1½ cups instant malted milk powder
6 ounces powdered non-dairy creamer
Marshmallows or whipped cream

Combine nonfat dry milk powder, powdered sugar, cocoa powder, malted milk powder and creamer in a large bowl. Stir until thoroughly combined. Store cocoa in an airtight container. Makes about 16 cups. For each individual serving, place ⅓ cup cocoa mixture in a mug and add ¾ cup boiling water. Stir to dissolve. Top with marshmallows or a dollop of whipped cream.

Warm and Cozy Cider

8 cups apple cider or apple juice
10 ounces frozen raspberries or sliced strawberries
4 inches stick cinnamon
1½ teaspoons whole cloves
1 large apple
Cinnamon sticks

Combine cider or juice, raspberries or strawberries, cinnamon and cloves in a large saucepan. Bring to a boil; reduce heat. Cover and simmer for 10 minutes. Strain through a sieve lined with 100% cotton cheesecloth. To serve pour warm cider into 8 heat-proof glasses or cups. Cut ⅛-inch thick slices from apple then cut into holiday shapes. Float a shape in each mug of cider and garnish with a cinnamon stick. Makes 8 servings.

Christmas Wassail

32 ounces cranberry juice cocktail
1 cup water
⅓ cup frozen pineapple-orange juice concentrate, thawed
2 or more sticks of cinnamon
2 whole cloves
Orange peel strips
Stick cinnamon

In a large saucepan stir together the cranberry juice cocktail, water, juice concentrate, cinnamon stick and cloves. Bring to a boil; reduce heat. Cover and simmer for 10 minutes. Using a slotted spoon, remove cinnamon and cloves from mixture. Transfer the juice mixture to a small punch bowl when slightly cooled and garnish with orange peel and cinnamon. Makes 10 servings.

Spiced Apple Cider

2 quarts apple cider or unsweetened apple juice
½ cup firmly packed brown sugar
1 cinnamon stick
½ teaspoon ground nutmeg
¼ teaspoon ground allspice
2 tablespoons lemon juice
1 cup water
2 red delicious apples

In large saucepan combine apple cider, brown sugar, cinnamon stick, nutmeg and allspice. Bring to a boil; reduce heat and simmer 30 minutes. Remove cinnamon stick. Meanwhile, in a small bowl, combine lemon juice and water. Slice apples into thin slices; dip in lemon juice mixture to prevent discoloring. Place cider mixture in heatproof punch bowl. Garnish with apple slices. Makes 8 servings.

Warm Mocha Mix

½ cup instant espresso granules or coffee granules
¼ cup unsweetened cocoa
¼ cup non-dairy creamer
6 tablespoons powdered sugar

Combine all ingredients; mix well. To serve, spoon 1 to 2 tablespoons mix into cup. Add ¾ cup boiling water; stir to dissolve. Garnish with whipped cream and a pinch of cocoa. Serve immediately.

Cozy Fruit Tea

5½ cups boiling water
4 tea bags
¼ teaspoon cinnamon
10 whole cloves
¼ to ½ cup sugar
½ cup orange juice
2 to 4 tablespoons lemon juice

In a large teapot, pour boiling water over tea bags, cinnamon and cloves. Cover and steep for 5 minutes. Strain tea into a saucepan. Stir in sugar, orange juice and lemon juice.   Cook over medium heat until mixture simmers. Serve immediately. Makes 8 servings.

Traditional Eggnog

6 beaten egg yolks
2¼ to 2½ cups milk
⅓ cup sugar
1 teaspoon vanilla
1 cup whipping cream
2 tablespoons sugar
Ground nutmeg

Combine egg yolks, milk and sugar in a large, heavy saucepan. Cook and stir over medium heat until mixture coats a metal spoon. Remove from heat. Cool quickly by placing pan in a sink or bowl of ice water and stirring for 1 to 2 minutes. Stir in the vanilla; chill for 4 to 24 hours. At serving time, whip the cream and sugar until soft peaks form. Transfer chilled egg mixture to a punch bowl. Fold in whipped cream mixture. Sprinkle each serving with nutmeg. Makes about 10 servings.

Poinsettia Punch

3 cups lemon-lime soft drink, chilled
2 cups cranberry juice cocktail, chilled
½ cup orange liqueur
1 teaspoon almond extract

In a 2-quart pitcher, stir together all ingredients. Pour into crystal goblets. To garnish, drop a few fresh cranberries into each goblet. Makes 8 servings.

Sparkling Citrus Punch

46-ounce can pineapple juice
1½ cups orange juice
¾ cup lemon juice
¼ cup lime juice
1¼ cups sugar
2 bottles ginger ale, chilled

Combine first 5 ingredients, stirring until sugar dissolves. Pour into ice cube trays; cover and freeze until firm. Place four juice cubes in each glass. Pour 1 cup ginger ale over cubes; stir until slushy. Makes about 17 servings.

Mint Refresher

1 jar mint jelly
2 cups water
3 cups unsweetened pineapple juice
½ cup lemon juice
1 can ginger ale, chilled

Combine jelly and water in saucepan; cook over low heat, stirring frequently, until jelly melts. Let cool. Stir in juices; cover and chill. Before serving stir in ginger ale. Makes 7 cups.

Boiled Custard

1 quart milk
4 large eggs
¾ cup sugar
2 tablespoons all-purpose flour
2 teaspoons vanilla

Cook milk over medium heat for 10 minutes or until hot. Combine remaining ingredients in a separate bowl, beating with a wire whisk until blended. Gradually stir 1 cup hot milk into egg mixture; add to remaining hot milk, stirring constantly. Cook over medium heat, stirring constantly for 6 to 8 minutes or until mixture begins to thicken and reaches 180 degrees. Remove from heat and pour through a strainer into a bowl or container; chill. Makes 5 cups.

Easy Boiled Custard

One 3¾ ounce package French vanilla instant pudding mix
4 cups milk
½ cup sugar
1 teaspoon vanilla
One 8 ounce carton Cool Whip
Whipped topping

Add pudding mix, sugar and vanilla to milk. Stir until smooth. Fold in whipped topping. Chill until very, very cold.

Curtis Grace
Cooking with Curtis Grace

Breads

Banana Nut Bread

1 teaspoon cinnamon
1 cup sugar
1 cup self-rising flour
1 stick softened butter
3 mashed bananas
1 egg, beaten
1 teaspoon baking soda, dissolved in ½ teaspoon water
1 teaspoon vanilla
1 cup pecans

Mix dry ingredients, then add butter, bananas and egg. Mix well. Stir in dissolved baking soda and vanilla. Mix and add pecans. Pour into a greased and floured loaf pan and bake 1 hour at 350 degrees.

Zucchini Bread

3 eggs
1 cup oil
2 cups sugar
3 teaspoons vanilla
2 cups grated, peeled zucchini
3 cups all-purpose flour
1 teaspoon salt
1 teaspoon baking soda
3 teaspoons cinnamon
1 teaspoon baking powder
4¼ cups nuts

Grease and flour two loaf pans. Beat eggs until light. Add oil, sugar, vanilla and zucchini. Mix well. Add flour, salt, baking soda, cinnamon and baking powder. Mix well and add nuts. Pour into pans and bake at 350 degrees for 1 hour.

Marilyn's Monkey Bread

Two 12-ounce cans biscuits
⅓ cup sugar
1 teaspoon cinnamon
Nuts
¾ stick margarine or butter
1½ teaspoons cinnamon
½ cup brown sugar

Preheat oven to 350 degrees. Put biscuits, sugar and cinnamon in a plastic bag and shake until well coated. Grease bundt pan. Scatter nuts in the bottom. Boil butter, cinnamon and brown sugar. Place biscuits in a tube pan and pour butter mixture over top. Bake for 10 to 15 minutes.

Easy and Delicious Rolls

1 package dry yeast
2 tablespoons warm water
4 cups self-rising flour
1 cup hot water
6 tablespoon shortening
1 egg
1 teaspoon salt
¼ cup sugar

Dissolve yeast in water. Mix all ingredients. Roll out and cut. Place in well buttered pan. Let rise in a warm place for at least 2 hours. When ready bake at 350 degrees until done.

Mayonnaise Rolls

1 cup self-rising flour
½ cup milk
2 tablespoons mayonnaise

Combine all ingredients and mix well. Fill greased muffin tins ⅔ full. Bake at 375 degrees for 14 minutes. Makes 6 rolls.

Quick and Easy Yeast Rolls

4¼ cups all-purpose flour, divided
3 tablespoons sugar
¼ teaspoon baking soda
1 teaspoon salt
2 packages dry yeast
1½ cups buttermilk
¼ cup water
¼ cup butter or margarine
Melted butter or margarine

Combine 1¼ cups flour, sugar, baking soda, salt and yeast in a mixing bowl; set aside. Combine buttermilk, water and ¼ cup butter in saucepan; heat to 120 to 130 degrees, stirring well. Add to flour mixture. Beat at medium speed 4 minutes. Gradually add remaining flour, mixing well. Turn dough out on a floured surface, and knead until smooth and elastic. Place in a greased bowl, turning to grease top. Cover and let rise in a warm place, about 30 minutes or double in bulk. Punch dough down and shape into 1½ inch balls. Place on a greased cookie sheet; cover and let rise in a warm place. Bake at 400 degrees for 15 to 20 minutes. Brush with melted butter. Makes 2 dozen rolls.

Verne's Delicious White Rolls

5 to 6 cups bread flour
3 tablespoons sugar
2 teaspoons salt
2 packages active dry yeast
2 cups water
¼ cup oil
Margarine or butter, melted

In a large bowl, lightly spoon 2 cups flour; add sugar, salt and yeast. Mix well. In small saucepan, heat water and oil until very warm (120 to 130 degrees). Add warm liquid to flour mixture. Blend at low speed until moistened; beat 3 minutes at medium speed. By hand, stir in an additional 2½ to 3 cups flour until dough pulls cleanly away from sides of bowl. On floured surface, knead in 1½ to 2 cups flour until dough is smooth and elastic; about 10 minutes. Place dough in greased bowl; cover loosely with cloth towel. Let rise in warm place until light and doubled in size, about 1 to 1½ hours.

Punch down dough several times to remove all air bubbles. Divide dough in half. Cover dough with inverted bowl and allow to rest on counter for 15 minutes. Grease two 13x9-inch pans. Divide each half of dough into 16 equal pieces. Shape each piece into a ball, pulling edges under to make a smooth top. Place 16 balls, smooth side up in each greased pan. Cover and let rise 30 to 45 minutes or until doubled in size. Bake at 400 degrees for 15 to 20 minutes or until brown. Makes 32 rolls.

Quick Biscuits

3 cups self-rising flour
½ cup shortening
1 cup milk

Put flour in a large bowl and cut in shortening with a fork until mixture looks like coarse corn meal. Add milk and blend lightly until flour is moist and dough pulls away from sides of bowl. Turn out onto a lightly floured surface. Knead lightly and roll out. Cut out biscuits and place on a lightly greased pan and brush tops with butter or margarine. Bake at 450 degrees for 12 to 15 minutes. Makes about 3 dozen biscuits.

Mexican Cornbread

1 cup cornmeal
1 cup milk
2 eggs, beaten
¾ teaspoon salt
½ teaspoon soda
½ cup bacon drippings or cooking oil
1 can cream-style corn
1 pound hamburger with chili powder
1 pound cheddar cheese, shredded
1 onion, chopped
4 to 5 jalapeño peppers, chopped

Combine cornmeal, milk, eggs, salt, soda, oil and corn. Sauté hamburger until lightly brown; drain. Pour half of cornmeal batter into a greased 9x13x2-inch pan. Sprinkle with cheese. Crumble hamburger over cheese and sprinkle with onion and peppers. Pour remaining cornmeal batter over top. Bake at 350 degrees for 50 minutes. Makes 10 to 12 servings.

Cheese Bread

2 cups biscuit mix
½ cup grated cheddar cheese
2 tablespoons minced onion
1 egg, beaten
½ cup plus 2 tablespoons milk
½ cup grated cheddar cheese
Poppy seeds

Mix biscuit mix, cheese and onion. Add egg and milk. Stir until moist.
Spread in greased cake or bread pan. Top with cheese and lots of poppy seeds.
Bake at 400 degrees for 20 minutes.

Wheat Swirl Bread

4½ to 5 cups all-purpose flour
2 packages active dry yeast
2 cups milk
½ cup honey
¼ cup butter
1 teaspoon salt
2 egg whites
1 cup whole wheat flour
½ cup rye flour
½ cup toasted wheat germ
¼ cup butter, softened
⅔ cup packed brown sugar

Combine 2 cups all-purpose flour and yeast. Heat milk, honey, butter and salt until warm. Add to flour mixture; add egg whites. Beat on low 30 seconds, scraping bowl constantly. Beat on high 3 minutes. Stir in wheat and rye flours, wheat germ and as much remaining all-purpose flour as you can. Turn onto a floured surface. Knead until smooth and elastic, 6 to 8 minutes. Place into a greased bowl. Cover; let rise in a warm place until nearly double. Punch dough down. Turn onto a floured surface; divide in half. Cover; let rest 10 minutes. Roll half to a 15-inch square. Spread with butter; sprinkle with brown sugar. Roll up jelly-roll style; cut in half. Seal ends; place into 4 greased loaf pans. Cover; let rise in a warm place until double. Bake at 350° 30 minutes or loaves sound hollow when tapped. Remove from pans immediately.

Whole Wheat Sourdough Bread

3¾ to 4¼ cups all-purpose flour
1 package active dry yeast
1½ cups warm water
3 tablespoons brown sugar
3 tablespoons olive oil
1½ teaspoons salt
1½ cups whole wheat sourdough starter, at room temperature
2 cups whole wheat flour
1 tablespoons cornmeal

Combine 2 cups flour and yeast; set aside. In a separate bowl stir together warm water, brown sugar, oil and salt; add to flour mixture. Add sourdough starter. Beat on low 30 seconds, scraping sides of bowl. Beat on high 3 minutes. Using a spoon, stir in whole wheat flour and as much of the remaining flour as you can.

On a lightly floured surface, knead dough until smooth and elastic, 8 to 10 minutes. Shape dough into a ball. Place dough in a greased bowl, turning once to grease surface of the dough. Cover, let rise in a warm place until double. Punch dough down. Turn onto a lightly floured surface. Divide in half. Cover and let rest 10 minutes.

Shape dough into 2 long loaves, each about 12x4 inches wide. Lightly grease 1 or 2 large baking sheets; sprinkle with cornmeal. Place loaves on sheets.

Cover with a warm damp cloth. Let rise in a warm place until double or you may let dough rise, covered, in the refrigerator for 12 hours. Place a pan of warm water on the lowest rack of oven. Preheat oven to 375 degrees. Use a serrated knife to make 4 or 5 diagonal slashes about ½ deep across the tops of the loaves. Place baking sheets on rack above pan of water. Bake, uncovered, 40 to 45 minutes or until bread sounds hollow when tapped. Cool on a wire rack. Makes 2 loaves.

Sourdough Wheat Starter

1 package dry yeast
½ cup warm water
1 cup all-purpose flour
1 cup whole wheat flour
3 tablespoons sugar
1 teaspoon salt
2 cups warm water

Combine yeast and warm water in a glass measuring cup; let stand 5 minutes. Combine flours, sugar and salt in a nonmetal bowl; gradually stir in warm water. Add yeast mixture. Cover loosely with plastic wrap; let stand in a warm place for 72 hours, stirring 2 or 3 times daily. Refrigerate and stir once daily. Replenish or use within 11 days. Makes 3 cups.

Breakfast

&

Brunch

Christmas Breakfast Muffins

1¾ cups all-purpose flour
⅔ cup chopped hazelnuts or pecans, toasted
¼ cup sugar
2 teaspoons baking powder
½ teaspoon salt
1 beaten egg
¾ cup milk
⅓ cup cooking oil
⅓ cup chopped hazelnuts or pecans

Grease six 3½-inch muffin cups (or twelve 2½-inch muffin cups) or line them with paper baking cups. Set aside. Stir together the flour, toasted nuts, sugar, baking powder and salt. Make a well in the center of the dry mixture. In another bowl combine the egg, milk and cooking oil. Add the egg mixture all at once to the dry mixture. Stir just until moistened. Spoon the batter into the prepared muffin cups, filling each full. Sprinkle with nuts. Bake the large muffins in a 350 degree oven for 25 to 27 minutes (the small in a 400 degree oven for 18 to 20 minutes) or until golden brown. Remove the muffins and cool on a wire rack. Makes 6 or 12 muffins.

Delicious Pumpkin Muffins

4 cups all-purpose flour
1¾ teaspoons baking soda
1 teaspoon salt
½ teaspoon baking powder
2¾ cups sugar
1 tablespoon ground cinnamon
1 tablespoon ground nutmeg
1 tablespoon ground cloves
1¼ cups raisins
¾ cup chopped walnuts
4 large eggs, lightly beaten
2½ cups mashed cooked pumpkin
1 cup vegetable oil
1 cup water

Combine first 10 ingredients. Make a well in center of mixture. Combine eggs and remaining ingredients; add to dry ingredients, stirring just until moistened. Spoon into paper-lined muffin tins, filling two-thirds full. Bake at 375 degrees for 20 minutes. Remove from pans immediately. Makes 3½ dozen.

Paula's Cranberry Raisin Muffins

2 cups raisin bran cereal
1 cup skim milk
½ cup brown sugar
1¼ cups self-rising flour
½ teaspoon soda
½ teaspoon cinnamon
½ container plain yogurt
⅓ cup whole cranberry sauce

Mix cereal and milk and let stand. Mix sugar, flour, soda, cinnamon; add cereal and mix. Blend in yogurt and sauce. Bake at 400 degrees for 20 minutes. Makes 12 muffins.

Orange Delight Muffins

Two 6-ounce cans frozen orange juice concentrate, thawed
½ cup sugar
4 tablespoons oil
2 eggs, beaten
4 cups biscuit mix
1 cup orange marmalade
1 cup granola or chopped, toasted pecans

Combine juice, sugar, oil and eggs. Add biscuit mix, marmalade and nuts.
Pour into 12 greased muffin tins and bake at 400 degrees for 20 minutes.

Apple Coffee Cake

1½ cups vegetable oil
2 cups sugar
3 eggs
3 cups all-purpose flour
1 teaspoon baking soda
½ teaspoon salt
2 teaspoons vanilla
3 cups apples, peeled and finely chopped
1 cup coconut
1 cup chopped nuts
¾ cup light brown sugar
¼ cup margarine
½ cup milk

Preheat oven to 325 degrees. Mix oil and sugar. Add eggs, flour, soda, salt and vanilla. Beat until well blended. Stir in apples, coconut and nuts. Place in a greased and floured tube pan. Bake 1½ hours.

Topping: mix brown sugar, margarine and milk in small saucepan. Heat and stir until blended. Boil 2 minutes. Pour over hot cake and allow topping to soak in. Let cake cool completely before removing it from pan.

Biscotti

6 eggs
2 teaspoons vanilla
½ teaspoon almond extract
4 cups flour
1¾ cups sugar
2 teaspoons baking soda
½ teaspoon salt
1½ cups toasted almonds

Beat eggs, vanilla and almond extract. Combine flour, sugar, baking soda and salt. Add egg mixture and mix until blended. Fold in nuts. Divide dough into 4 portions. On greased, floured baking sheet, pat out dough into 4 logs, ½-inch thick, 1½-inches wide and 12-inches long. Space at least 2-inches apart. Bake at 300 degrees for 50 minutes or until golden brown. Cool for 5 minutes. Cut at a 45 degree angle, ½-inch thick. Lay slices flat and rebake at 275 degrees for 20 to 25 minutes or until toasted. Turn once to toast both sides.

Good Morning Sweet Rolls

2 cups milk
⅓ cup sugar
2 teaspoons salt
½ cup shortening
2 eggs
1 package dry yeast
¼ cup lukewarm water
6 cups all-purpose flour

Scald milk and add sugar, salt and shortening; allow to cook until lukewarm. Beat the eggs well and add to mixture. Dissolve yeast in lukewarm water and add to mixture. Add enough flour to mixture to make a soft dough. Knead dough until smooth and elastic. Place in a well greased bowl; cover with a cloth and set in a warm place until dough has doubled. Shape rolls and place in a greased pan. Set in warm place, allow to rise until double in size and bake at 400 degrees for 15 to 20 minutes.

Best French Toast

6 eggs
1 cup milk
1 teaspoon salt
⅔ cup vegetable oil
1 teaspoon vanilla
½ cup sugar
1 teaspoon nutmeg
1 teaspoon cinnamon
8 slices bread, sliced 1-inch thick

Combine all ingredients except bread. Place bread in a greased baking dish and pour egg mixture over. Cover and refrigerate overnight. Bake at 450 degrees for 10 minutes; turn and bake 10 minutes more.

Breakfast Casserole

6 slices bread, cut into cubes
Nonstick spray coating
½ pound pork or turkey sausage
1 medium green pepper, chopped
½ cup mushrooms, chopped
½ cup onions, chopped
1 cup shredded sharp cheddar cheese
1 can cream of mushroom soup
2 eggs, well beaten
1 cup evaporated milk
¾ teaspoon dry mustard
½ teaspoon salt
⅛ teaspoon pepper

Place bread cubes in a large, shallow pan. Bake in a 350 degree oven for 8 to 10 minutes or until toasted, stirring once. Spray a 9x12-inch baking dish with nonstick spray. Place half of the bread cubes in the baking dish; set aside. Meanwhile, in a large skillet, cook sausage, green pepper, onions and mushrooms over medium-high heat until sausage is brown. Drain off fat. Spoon mixture on top of bread cubes in dish. Sprinkle with half of the shredded cheese. Top with remaining bread. In a medium mixing bowl combine soup, eggs, milk, mustard, salt and pepper. Pour over bread, pressing down cubes with back of spoon to moisten. Cover; chill for at least 2 hours or for up to 24 hours. Bake at 350 degrees for 45 minutes. Sprinkle with remaining cheese. Bake 2 to 3 minutes more. Let stand for 5 minutes before serving.

Christmas Brunch Casserole

2 cans refrigerated crescent rolls
¼ cup margarine or butter
½ cup chopped green onions or onion
⅓ cup all-purpose flour
¼ teaspoon dried thyme
¼ teaspoon pepper
1 can chicken broth
1½ cups mixed vegetables
2 cups diced, cooked ham
6 hard boiled eggs, chopped
1 egg, beaten
1 to 2 teaspoons sesame seed

Preheat oven to 375 degrees. Separate one can of crescent rolls into 2 long rectangles. Keep remaining can refrigerated. Press rectangles over bottom of a 13x9-inch baking dish. Bake at 375 degrees for 8 to 13 minutes or until golden brown. Meanwhile, melt margarine over medium heat. Add onion; cook and stir until crisp-tender. Stir in flour, thyme, pepper and chicken broth. Cook 3 to 4 minutes or until mixture boils and thickens, stirring constantly. Reduce to low heat. Stir in vegetables; cook 4 to 6 minutes or until vegetables are crisp-tender. Stir in ham and hard boiled eggs; cook 3 to 5 minutes or until thoroughly heated. Spoon vegetable mixture over partially baked crust. Unroll other can of crescent rolls and make a 13x9-inch rectangle. Put on top of casserole and bake 20 to 25 minutes or until golden brown. Makes 8 servings.

Brunch Torte

2 frozen pie crusts, thawed
1 cup shredded cheddar cheese
¾ pound thinly sliced cooked ham
1½ cups thinly sliced, unpeeled red potatoes
1 medium onion, sliced
9 ounces frozen spinach, thawed and squeezed to drain
1 egg
1 tablespoon water

Preheat oven to 375 degrees. Put cookie sheet in oven to heat. Press one crust on bottom and up sides of a 9-inch pie pan. Sprinkle ⅓ cup cheese on bottom of crust. Top with half of ham, half of potatoes and half of onion slices. Distribute spinach evenly over onion. Top with ⅓ cup cheese and remaining ham, potatoes and onion. Sprinkle remaining cheese over onion. Gently press mixture into pan. Top with second crust; fold over top edge of bottom crust and pinch edges to seal. Cut slits in top crust. Mix egg and water and brush top with mixture. Place torte on hot cookie sheet and bake at 375 degrees for 45 to 60 minutes or until crust is golden brown and filling is thoroughly heated. Makes 8 servings.

Glazed Apples with Canadian Bacon

½ cup firmly packed brown sugar
⅛ teaspoon pepper
1 tablespoon lemon juice
2 large cooking apples, cored and each cut into 16 wedges
1 pound sliced Canadian bacon

Combine brown sugar, pepper and lemon juice and cook over medium heat until brown sugar is melted. Add apples; cook 5 to 6 minutes or until tender, stirring occasionally. Place apples on a serving platter. In same skillet cook Canadian bacon 1 to 2 minutes or until hot, turning once. Arrange on platter with apples. Spoon remaining liquid over apples and Canadian bacon. Makes 8 servings.

Soups

&

Salads

Oyster Stew

8 ounces frozen mixed broccoli, cauliflower and carrots
1 small onion, cut in thin wedges
½ cup water
½ teaspoon instant chicken bouillon granules
⅛ teaspoon ground white pepper
1 bay leaf
3½ cups evaporated skim milk
1 pint shucked oysters or 16 ounces whole oysters

Cut up any large vegetables. In a 3-quart saucepan combine the vegetables, onion, water, bouillon granules, white pepper and bay leaf. Bring to a boil. Reduce heat. Cover and simmer for 5 to 7 minutes or until the vegetables are crisp-tender. Do not drain. Stir in the evaporated milk. Heat all the way through. Add the undrained oysters to the vegetable mixture. Cook over a medium heat for about 5 minutes or until the edges of the oysters curl, stirring frequently. Remove the bay leaf. Makes 6 servings.

Tasty Potato Soup

8 cups sliced potatoes
1 medium onion, chopped
Water
1½ sticks margarine
2 large cans evaporated milk
Parsley flakes

Put potatoes and onion in a 4-quart saucepan. Add water to cover and cook until tender. Remove from heat. Using a potato masher, break potatoes into smaller pieces. Add margarine and milk. Reheat until margarine has melted, stirring constantly. When serving, sprinkle with parsley. Makes 6 servings.

Spicy Tomato Warm-up

46-ounce can spicy vegetable juice
3 beef flavored bouillon cubes
1 tablespoon Worcestershire sauce
3 tablespoons lemon juice
⅛ teaspoon pepper
¼ to ½ teaspoon hot sauce

Combine all ingredients in a large saucepan; cook over medium heat until bouillon cubes dissolve. Serve warm. Makes 5½ cups.

Mushroom Soup

4 medium onions, minced
2 cloves garlic, minced
¼ cup butter or margarine
2 pounds fresh mushrooms, coarsely chopped
2 cups whipping cream
2 cups beef broth
1 cup grated Parmesan cheese
1 cup sliced almonds, toasted
Chopped fresh parsley

Sauté onion and garlic in butter in a Dutch oven over medium heat until onion is tender. Add mushrooms; cook over low heat 10 minutes or until tender. Gradually add cream and broth; continue to cook until heated through. Do not boil. Sprinkle cheese, almonds and parsley over each serving. Makes 2½ quarts.

Pam's Cream of Vegetable Soup

2 tablespoons butter
1 clove garlic, chopped
1 medium onion, sliced
¼ head of cauliflower, broken
2 carrots, chopped
2 stalks celery, chopped
6 asparagus stalks, chopped
1 leek, chopped
1 large potato, peeled and chopped
1 cup chopped spinach
Salt and pepper, to taste
1 quart chicken stock
Pinch of cayenne pepper
1 cup heavy cream
3 tablespoons flour
1 tablespoon chopped parsley
1 tablespoon Parmesan cheese

Heat butter in a soup pot; add onion and garlic and sauté for 3 minutes. Add vegetables, salt and pepper to the pot and cook 5 to 6 minutes. Add the chicken stock and cayenne; simmer 25 to 30 minutes. Mix the cream and flour until smooth. Pour slowly into the soup, stirring constantly. Simmer until begins thickening. Serve with parsley and grated Parmesan cheese on top.

Having Company Chili

1 pound ground beef
1 pound hot smoked sausage, sliced
1 cup chopped onion
28 ounces pinto beans, undrained
28 ounces whole tomatoes, undrained and chopped
½ cup ketchup
1 tablespoon chili powder
2 teaspoons brown sugar
1 teaspoon brown mustard
½ teaspoon salt

Combine ground beef, sausage and onion and cook until beef is browned, stirring to crumble meat. Drain.

Drain pinto beans, reserving liquid. Add liquid to sausage mix; stir in remaining ingredients except beans. Cover and simmer 45 minutes. Stir in beans. Cook 15 more minutes. Makes 3 quarts.

Vegetable-Shrimp Bisque

1 pound zucchini, thinly sliced
1 cup thinly sliced carrot
½ cup chopped celery
½ cup sliced green onion
½ cup chicken broth
1¾ cups skim milk
1 can cream of mushroom soup
½ cup plain yogurt
1 can small shrimp, drained and rinsed
1 tablespoon dry white wine

Combine vegetables and chicken broth; cover and simmer 15 to 20 minutes or until vegetables are tender. In a blender mix half of vegetable mixture until smooth and repeat with remaining vegetables. Return to pan; stir in remaining ingredients. Cook over low heat, stirring constantly, until thoroughly heated. Makes 10 cups.

Crowd Pleasing White Chili

2 to 3 large cans white northern beans
6 chicken breasts, cooked and shredded or chopped
Broth from chicken
2 onions, chopped
4 cloves garlic
Chili powder, to taste or one package chili seasoning
1 to 2 cans cream of mushroom soup

Put all ingredients in crock pot and cook on low as long as desired. When serving, top with salsa and sour cream.

Verne's Frozen Fruit Medley

29-ounce can fruit cocktail
1 package lemon-flavored gelatin
1 cup hot water
2 tablespoons lemon juice
6 ounces cream cheese
½ cup mayonnaise or salad dressing
1½ cups tiny marshmallows
¼ cup drained, quartered maraschino cherries
1 cup heavy cream, whipped

Drain fruit cocktail, reserving 1 cup syrup. Dissolve gelatin in hot water; add reserved syrup and lemon juice. Chill until partially set. Soften cream cheese, add mayonnaise and beat until smooth. Add cheese mixture to gelatin mixture, mixing well. Stir in fruit cocktail, marshmallows and cherries. Fold in whipped cream. Pour into oblong dish. Freeze several hours or overnight. Slice and place on top of lettuce. Makes 12 servings.

Potluck Pasta Salad

8 ounces spiral pasta
½ cup vegetable oil
¼ cup vinegar
1 large clove garlic, minced
2 tablespoons lemon juice
2 teaspoons prepared mustard
2 teaspoons Worcestershire sauce
1 teaspoon salt
Dash of pepper
1 cup snow peas, ends and strings removed
2 cups broccoli flowerets
2 cups mushrooms, sliced
1 cup cauliflower flowerets
1 cup halved cherry tomatoes

Cook pasta according to package directions; drain. Meanwhile, in screwtop jar, combine oil, vinegar, garlic, lemon juice, mustard, Worcestershire sauce, salt and pepper; shake well. In a large bowl, combine hot pasta with dressing; mix well. Add vegetables; toss to coat. Refrigerate, covered. Makes 8 servings.

Chilled Broccoli Salad

1 bunch broccoli, chopped
1 purple onion, chopped
¼ cup raisins
6 slices bacon, fried crisp and crumbled
¼ cup sugar
2 tablespoons vinegar
1 cup mayonnaise

Put broccoli, onion, raisins and bacon in bowl. Add sugar and vinegar to mayonnaise. Mix well and pour over broccoli mix. Stir well and chill overnight before serving.

Crunchy Salad

1 cup uncooked rice
11 ounces mandarin oranges, drained
1 cup chopped green onion
1 cup sliced celery
8 ounces water chestnuts, drained
3½ ounces sliced mushrooms, drained
¼ cup rice vinegar
¼ cup vegetable oil
¼ cup soy sauce
Lettuce leaves

Cook rice according to directions, omitting salt. Cool. Combine rice and next five ingredients, tossing lightly. Combine vinegar, oil and soy sauce; pour over rice mixture, and lightly toss. Chill thoroughly and serve on lettuce leaves. Makes 10 to 12 servings.

Delectable Ambrosia

1 quart orange sections
1 cup sliced bananas
½ cup pineapple bits
½ cup coconut
½ cup maraschino cherries
½ cup pecans, chopped
1 cup sugar

Mix all ingredients thoroughly. Chill and serve in grapefruit or orange halves scooped out and placed on lettuce leaves. Serves 6.

Beautiful Cranberry Mold

1½ cups water
2 packages raspberry gelatin
1 can whole cranberries
1 can apple sauce
1 can crushed pineapple
Nuts

Boil water. Mix in gelatin and add remaining ingredients. Pour into lightly greased or sprayed mold (or use a bundt pan) and let set. Unmold onto lettuce leaves and serve on a platter for a beautiful salad.

Side Items

Green Bean Casserole

2 cans French-style green beans
1 can cream of mushroom soup
½ cup milk
1 can fried onion rings
Black pepper, to taste

Drain green beans. Add soup and milk, stirring well. Add half the can of onion rings and black pepper. Stir together and pour into a 1½-quart baking dish. Bake at 350 degrees for 30 to 35 minutes or until bubbly. Remove and add the remaining onion rings and bake 5 more minutes.

Great Oven-Roasted Potatoes

4 baking potatoes
2 tablespoons butter, melted
2 teaspoons paprika
1 teaspoon salt
½ teaspoon pepper

Peel potatoes and cut into large chunks. Place in a shallow baking pan. Pour butter over potatoes and add paprika, salt and pepper. Shake until well coated. Bake uncovered at 350 degrees for 45 to 60 minutes.

Delicious Corn Pudding

¼ cup sugar
3 tablespoons all-purpose flour
2 teaspoons baking powder
2 teaspoons salt
6 large eggs
2 cups whipping cream
½ cup butter or margarine, melted
6 cups whole kernel or shoepeg corn

Combine first four ingredients. Beat eggs with a fork. Stir in whipping cream and butter. Gradually add sugar mixture, stirring until smooth; stir in corn. Pour mixture into a lightly greased 13x9x2-inch baking dish. Bake at 350 degrees for 45 minutes or until mixture is set. Let stand 5 minutes. Makes 8 servings.

Scalloped Oysters

1 quart oysters, undrained
5 cups butter crackers, crushed
½ teaspoon salt
½ teaspoon ground red pepper
2 teaspoons Worcestershire sauce
2 cups half and half
¼ cup butter, cut into pieces

Drain oysters, reserving 3 tablespoons of liquid. Place half of cracker crumbs in a greased 13x9x2-inch baking dish. Arrange oysters over crumbs; sprinkle with salt, pepper and Worcestershire sauce. Top with remaining crumbs; drizzle with reserved liquid and half and half. Top with butter. Bake at 400 degrees for 30 minutes. Makes 8 servings.

Buttermilk and Basil Mashed Potatoes

3½ pounds potatoes, peeled and cut into 1-inch cubes
1 onion, chopped
3 stalks celery, cut in half
12 cloves garlic, peeled
½ teaspoon salt
¾ cup cottage cheese
½ cup buttermilk
2 to 4 tablespoons chopped fresh basil
1 teaspoon salt
¼ teaspoon freshly ground pepper

Combine first 5 ingredients in a Dutch oven; add water to cover. Bring to a boil over high heat; reduce heat and simmer 20 minutes or until potatoes are tender. Drain; remove and discard celery. Mash potato mixture. In a separate bowl beat cottage cheese and buttermilk until smooth. Add cottage cheese mixture to potato mixture, stirring mixture thoroughly until smooth. Stir in basil, salt and pepper. Cook over low heat until thoroughly heated. Serve immediately. Makes 8 servings.

Broccoli with Stuffing

20 ounces frozen broccoli spears
1 cup shredded cheddar cheese
2 large eggs, lightly beaten
1 can cream of mushroom soup
½ cup mayonnaise or salad dressing
½ cup finely chopped onion
¾ cup herb-seasoned stuffing mix
2 tablespoons butter or margarine, melted

Cook broccoli according to package directions; drain. Arrange broccoli in a lightly greased 11x7x1½-inch baking dish. Sprinkle with cheese. Combine eggs and next 3 ingredients; spread over cheese. Combine stuffing mix and butter; sprinkle over casserole. Bake casserole at 350 degrees for 30 minutes or until thoroughly heated. Makes 8 servings.

Broccoli Supreme

Four 10-ounce packages frozen broccoli spears
2 tablespoons minced onion
2 tablespoons butter or margarine
16 ounces sour cream
2 teaspoons sugar
½ teaspoon red wine vinegar
½ teaspoon paprika
⅓ cup chopped salted peanuts

Cook broccoli according to directions; drain. Sauté onion in butter until tender. Remove from heat; stir in sour cream, sugar, vinegar and paprika. Arrange broccoli on serving dish. Spoon sauce over broccoli; sprinkle with peanuts. Makes 8 to 10 servings.

Traditional Scalloped Potatoes

5 to 6 large potatoes, peeled and sliced
1½ cups chicken broth
½ teaspoon salt
¼ teaspoon pepper
1 cup shredded Swiss cheese
3 tablespoons grated Parmesan cheese

Combine first 4 ingredients; bring to a boil. Cover, reduce heat and simmer 5 minutes. Remove potatoes from broth, reserving broth. Layer half of each potatoes and Swiss cheese in a lightly greased 2-quart casserole dish; repeat layers. Pour broth over top; sprinkle with Parmesan cheese. Cover and bake at 350 degrees for 55 minutes. Remove cover and bake 5 more minutes or until potatoes are tender. Makes 8 servings.

Spiced Holiday Cranberries

4 cups cranberries
2 cups water
3 cups sugar
1 teaspoon ground cinnamon
½ teaspoon ground cloves
Pinch of ginger

Wash cranberries and drain; set aside. Combine remaining ingredients; bring to a boil. Add cranberries; cook 7 to 10 minutes or until cranberry skins pop. Reduce heat and simmer 1 hour, stirring occasionally. Remove from heat and let cool. Chill until ready to serve. Make 2 cups.

Cauliflower Italiano

2 small heads cauliflower
3 tablespoons all-purpose flour
½ teaspoon garlic powder
½ teaspoon pepper
1 small onion, thinly sliced
3 tablespoons butter or margarine
1 cup sliced olives
2 cups shredded mozzarella cheese
½ cup grated Parmesan cheese
2 tablespoons chopped parsley
¼ cup dry white wine
¾ cup milk
Paprika

Steam cauliflower flowerets 10 minutes or until crisp-tender. Remove from heat. Combine flour, garlic powder and pepper; set aside. Arrange half of flowerets in a greased 2½-quart baking dish; top with half of onion slices. Sprinkle half of flour mixture over onion; dot with half of butter. Top with half each of olives and cheeses. Sprinkle with parsley. Repeat second layer. Combine wine and milk, stirring well. Pour over casserole. Sprinkle with paprika. Bake uncovered at 350 degrees for 40 minutes. Makes 6 to 8 servings.

Delicious Dressing

1½ cups chopped onion
1½ cups chopped celery
Broth from turkey or chicken
Large skillet of cornbread, crumbled
2 sticks butter
1 teaspoon sugar
1 teaspoon pepper
2 eggs, beaten
1 can cream of mushroom soup
1 can cream of chicken soup
1 teaspoon salt
1 teaspoon sage

Sauté onion and celery in butter. Pour broth over cornbread; mix and add remaining ingredients. Put in a crock pot and cook on high for 45 minutes to an hour. Reduce to low and cook for 4 hours, stirring occasionally.

Hot Hash Brown Casserole

32 ounces frozen hash brown potatoes
¾ cup butter, melted
½ cup chopped onion
1 can cream of chicken soup
8 ounces sour cream
1 cup cheddar cheese
2 cups corn flakes

Combine hash brown potatoes, butter, onion, soup, sour cream and cheese; stir well. Spoon into a greased 2½-quart casserole dish. Crush cereal and sprinkle over hash brown mixture. Bake at 350 degrees for 50 minutes. Makes 8 to 10 servings.

Sweet Potato Casserole

3 cups sweet potatoes, mashed
1 cup sugar
2 eggs, lightly beaten
1 teaspoon vanilla
½ cup butter
⅓ cup all-purpose flour
1 cup brown sugar
⅓ cup butter
⅓ cup flour

Mix sweet potatoes, sugar, eggs, vanilla, butter and flour. Pour into a 2-quart baking dish. Combine brown sugar and remaining butter and flour. Mix well and pour over sweet potatoes. Bake at 375 degrees for 30 minutes.

* For a special holiday touch slice 12 oranges in half and scoop out sections. Add small amount of orange to potato mixture. Spoon potato mixture into orange shells and top with marshmallows. May be frozen. When ready to serve place in a baking dish and bake at 375 degrees for 30 minutes.

* For a variation: raisins, coconut and/or nuts may be added to potato mixture.

Hot Cranberries and Apples

2 cups cranberries
3 cups apples, cut up
1 cup sugar
1 stick butter
1 cup quick oatmeal
1 cup brown sugar

Put cranberries and apples in a baking dish. Melt butter and sugar and stir in oatmeal and brown sugar. Stir and pour over cranberries and apples. Bake at 350 degrees for 1 hour.

Elegant Spinach Florentines

1 cup milk
1 cup flour
2 eggs
½ teaspoon salt
1 package frozen spinach, cooked and drained
⅔ cup mayonnaise
3 eggs
4-ounce can chopped mushrooms, drained
6 slices cooked, crumbled bacon
Salt and pepper
1½ cups or 6 ounces sharp cheddar cheese
3 tablespoons flour

Preheat oven to 350 degrees and grease muffin tins.

Prepare the crepe mixture by mixing milk, flour, eggs and salt and set in refrigerator for 30 minutes. Heat greased iron skillet, and pour in ¼ cup mixture. When done remove and place into greased muffin tins and allow edges to flop over sides.

Mix filling of spinach, mayonnaise, eggs, mushrooms, bacon, seasonings, cheese and flour and pour into crepes. Bake at 350 degrees for approximately 40 minutes.

Green Rice

1 stick margarine
½ cup finely chopped onion
½ cup finely chopped celery
1 package frozen chopped broccoli
½ cups cooked rice
1 small jar Cheez Whiz
1 can cream of celery soup

Melt margarine and sauté onion and celery. Combine with remaining ingredients in a 2-quart baking dish and bake at 350 degrees for 30 minutes or until golden and bubbly.

Entrees

Beef Bourguignon

One 4 to 5-pound boneless sirloin roast
1 cup Burgundy or dry red wine
1 cup water
2 cans cream of mushroom soup
1 package onion soup mix
2 cups mushrooms, sliced
1 cup chopped green pepper
1 pound pearl onions, peeled
½ teaspoon garlic powder
10 cherry tomatoes

Cut beef into cubes; place in a 2½-quart casserole. Combine wine, water, soup and soup mix; stir well and pour over beef. Stir in mushrooms; cover and bake at 325 degrees for 2 hours. Add green pepper, onions and garlic powder and bake an additional 30 minutes. Stir in cherry tomatoes. Serve over rice. Makes 10 to 12 servings.

On the Go Hamburger Casserole

1 pound ground beef
1 onion, chopped
6 potatoes, diced
1 can cream of mushroom soup
½ cup milk
2 tablespoons butter
1 pound Velveeta

Brown beef and onion. Boil potatoes separately. Mix beef, soup, milk , butter, Velveeta and potatoes in a covered casserole dish. Bake at 350 degrees for 20 minutes or until cheese is melted.

Mom's Meatballs

1 pound ground beef
1 package dry onion soup mix
2 eggs
2 pieces bread, soaked in milk
1 can beef broth
1 can cream of mushroom soup

Mix first four ingredients together. Roll into balls and brown. Drain and place in crockpot. Mix beef broth and soup together for gravy and pour over meatballs and cook on high for 2 hours.

Kid's Favorite Noodle Bake

4 cups medium egg noodles, cooked according to directions
1 pound ground beef
8 ounces tomato sauce
1 teaspoon salt
⅛ teaspoon pepper
¼ teaspoon garlic salt
2 cups sour cream
1 cup thinly sliced green onions
1 cup shredded cheddar cheese

Brown ground beef and drain. Add tomato sauce, salt, pepper and garlic salt to beef. Simmer uncovered for 5 minutes. In a separate dish, mix the noodles, sour cream and onions. Butter a 2-quart casserole dish. Layer noodles and beef alternately, starting with noodles and ending with beef. Sprinkle cheese on top. Bake at 350 degrees for 25 minutes. Makes 6 servings.

Company Pepper Steak

1½ pounds round steak
2 tablespoons olive oil
1 envelope onion soup mix
2 cups water
2 medium or 1 large green pepper, cut into thin strips
1½ tablespoons corn starch

Cut meat into thin strips 2-inches long. In a large skillet brown meat, turning frequently. Stir in onion soup and water. Cover and simmer 30 minutes or until meat is tender. Add green pepper. Blend corn starch with ½ cup water and stir into skillet until thickened. Serve with rice. Makes 4 to 6 servings.

Delicious Chicken Casserole

3 pound chicken, cooked
1 can cream of mushroom soup
1 can cream of celery soup
1 cup chicken broth
1 package stuffing mix
1 stick margarine

Debone chicken and set aside. Mix soups and broth well with a mixer. Melt butter and add stuffing mix. Set aside 1 cup of stuffing mixture. In a 9x13-inch pan layer ½ each of chicken, stuffing mixture and soup mixture. Repeat and top with stuffing mixture. Bake at 350 degrees for 30 minutes or until bubbly and brown.

Honey-Basil Chicken

1 cup raspberry vinegar
3 tablespoons Dijon mustard
2 tablespoons soy sauce
2 tablespoons honey
2 tablespoons minced basil
½ teaspoon dried thyme
Pinch of ground pepper
4 boneless, skinless chicken breasts

In a shallow glass baking dish, mix vinegar, mustard, soy sauce, honey, basil, thyme and pepper. Add the chicken and coat on both sides. Marinate at room temperature for 15 minutes. Transfer the chicken to the grill or broiling rack; reserve the marinade and place in a 1-quart saucepan. Grill or broil the chicken for 5 minutes on each side or until cooked through. While cooking chicken, boil marinade until reduced by half. Serve marinade over chicken. Make 4 servings.

Martha's Mexican Chicken Casserole

1 package Doritos, crushed
1 pound cooked chicken, diced
1 small can Rotel tomatoes
1 can cream of mushroom soup, add ¼ cup water
1 can cream of chicken soup, add ¼ cup water
1 medium onion, chopped or ¼ cup dried onion
½ pound cheddar cheese

Using a 9x13-inch casserole dish, layer ingredients. Start with half of Doritos, then all of the chicken, tomatoes, soups, onion and cheese. Spread remaining Doritos on top. Bake at 350 degrees for 30 minutes.

Potluck Chicken and Rice Casserole

4 pounds chicken breast
2 boxes wild rice
3 to 4 chopped onions
2 sticks butter
3 tablespoons flour
1½ cans mushroom soup
1 cup milk
1 large can sliced mushrooms
Salt and pepper, to taste
1 pound sharp cheese, grated

Cook and debone chicken. Cook rice. Sauté onions in butter; add flour, soup and milk. Add mushrooms and seasonings. Alternate layers of rice, chicken and mushroom filling. Cover top with cheese. Bake at 325 degrees for 20 to 30 minutes. Makes 20 servings.

Pam's Delicious Chicken

8 chicken breasts
½ cup flour
Salt and pepper, to taste
2 tablespoons olive oil
3 tablespoons butter
½ green pepper, thinly sliced
½ red pepper, thinly sliced
2 cloves garlic
8 large mushrooms, sliced
2 tomatoes, peeled and chopped
4 ounces white wine
2 tablespoons chopped parsley
½ cup chopped olives

Flatten and flour chicken breasts and season with salt and pepper. Heat olive oil and butter in a large frying pan and sauté chicken until brown. Remove chicken to a 15x10-inch baking dish. To the frying pan add peppers, garlic and mushrooms and cook for 4 minutes. Add tomatoes and wine and cook for 10 minutes. Pour over chicken in baking dish. Pour extra wine around chicken and bake at 325 degrees for 1 to 1½ hours. Garnish with parsley and olives.

Cranberry-Cornbread Stuffed Cornish Hens

6 ounces cornbread stuffing mix
½ cup water
½ cup thinly sliced celery
8 ounces cream cheese with chives and onions, softened
½ cup cranberries, fresh, frozen or canned, halved
¼ cup coarsely chopped pecans
4 Cornish hens
1 tablespoon vegetable oil

Combine seasoning packet from stuffing mix, water and celery in a large saucepan; bring to a boil. Cover, reduce heat and simmer 5 minutes. Add ¼ cup cream cheese, stirring until blended. Stir in stuffing mix, cranberries and pecans. Remove from heat; cover and let stand 5 minutes.

Loosen skin from hens without totally detaching; place remaining cream cheese under skin of hens. Lightly spoon stuffing mixture into hens; close opening with skewers. Place hens, breast side up, in a roasting pan; brush with oil. Bake at 350 degrees for 1 hour or until thermometer inserted in stuffing reads 165 degrees. Remove skewers and serve. Makes 4 servings.

Baked Ribs with Herbs

2½ or more pounds country style pork ribs
Soy sauce
Water
Thyme
Marjoram
Garlic
Basil
Rosemary

Boil ribs for 15 minutes and pour off excess water. Place in a shallow baking dish; mix equal amounts soy sauce and water and marinate ribs for at least 30 minutes. Pour marinade off and sprinkle herbs over ribs placed in a baking pan. Cover with foil and bake at 400 degrees for 30 minutes or until done. Serve garnished with fresh parsley.

Great Ginger Pork Stir-Fry

1 tablespoon soy sauce
1 tablespoon vinegar
1 teaspoon sesame oil
½ teaspoon ginger
1 clove garlic, minced
1 pound boneless pork loin, cut into ¾-inch cubes
1 tablespoon water
16 ounces frozen stir-fry vegetables

Blend soy sauce, vinegar, oil, ginger and garlic in shallow dish. Add pork; marinate for 10 minutes. Spray large, non-stick skillet with vegetable spray. Heat skillet over medium-high heat until hot. Add pork; stir-fry for 3 minutes. Stir water and vegetables into mixture. Cover and cook 5 minutes or until vegetables are crisp-tender. Makes 4 servings.

After Holidays Turkey Pot Pie

1 can mixed vegetables, drained
2 cans cream of potato soup
¼ cup milk
Salt and pepper, to taste
2 cups diced, cooked turkey
1 partially cooked pie shell
1 uncooked pie shell

Mix first 5 ingredients and pour into partially cooked pie shell; top with uncooked pie shell. Bake at 350 degrees for 25 minutes. Makes 4 servings.

*Note: Can use canned or homemade biscuits on top instead of pie shells.

Quick Turkey Divan

20 ounces frozen broccoli, cooked and drained
4 cups cooked, chopped turkey
2 cans cream of chicken soup
1 cup low-fat mayonnaise
½ cup shredded sharp cheese
1 can mushrooms
½ cup bread crumbs
Parmesan cheese
1 cup water chestnuts
1 teaspoon curry powder
½ stick butter, melted
Juice of 1 lemon

Arrange broccoli in a 9x13-inch baking dish. Place turkey on top of broccoli. Combine next 8 ingredients and pour over turkey. Top with melted butter and sprinkle lemon juice over all. Bake at 350 degrees for 1 hour and 15 minutes. Makes 6 to 8 servings.

Halibut with Soy Ginger Marinade

Soy Ginger Marinade:

¼ cup soy sauce
¼ cup water
¼ cup lemon juice
1 teaspoon minced garlic
1 tablespoon minced fresh ginger

4 filets of halibut
1 to 2 tablespoons butter
½ pound fresh mushrooms, stemmed and thinly sliced
½ pound oyster mushrooms, torn into pieces
½ pound domestic mushrooms, thinly sliced
2 tablespoons minced fresh ginger
2 tablespoons peeled and minced garlic
Salt and freshly ground pepper, to taste
2 teaspoons jalapeño chili pepper, minced
6 scallions, green tops only, cut into thin threads
4 tablespoons soft butter
1 tablespoon toasted sesame seeds

Mix soy ginger marinade ingredients together, pour over fish and marinate for 10 minutes. Heat butter in pan, add mushrooms and sauté until mushrooms begin to become crisp. Add ginger and garlic; cook another minute. Stir in chili pepper; add salt and pepper to taste. Cool.

Place baking sheet in oven and preheat to 425 degrees. Lay out 4 pieces of parchment about 18 inches long; divide fish among parchment (reserve the marinade and bring to a boil to save for later use), top with one quarter of mushrooms and one quarter of scallion greens; dot with butter and close packages. Place packages on hot baking sheet and bake 6 to 8 minutes, depending upon thickness of fish.

Divide packages among 4 plates, cut open, and sprinkle with toasted sesame seeds. Pass marinade separately. Makes 4 servings.

Spicy Cajun Dressing

1 pound hot sausage
1 pound mild sausage
1 large onion, chopped
1 large green pepper, chopped
3 stalks celery, chopped
2 envelopes instant chicken noodle soup mix
2 cups uncooked rice
6 cups water

Brown sausage, stirring to crumble; drain. Stir in remaining ingredients, mixing well. Place mixture in a 4½-quart casserole dish. Cover and bake at 350 degrees for 1 hour; uncover and bake an additional 15 to 20 minutes or until moisture is absorbed. Makes 12 to 15 servings.

Desserts

Red and Green Holiday Cake

Two baked 9-inch round white cake layers, cooled
2 cups boiling water
1 small package gelatin, red flavor
1 small package gelatin, lime flavor
12 ounces whipped topping

Place cake layers top sides up in 2 cake pans. Pierce cake with large fork at ½-inch intervals.

Stir 1 cup boiling water into each flavor gelatin, in separate bowls, for 2 minutes or until dissolved. Carefully pour red gelatin over one cake layer and the lime gelatin over the other. Refrigerate 3 hours. Dip cake pan in warm water 10 seconds and unmold on a serving plate. Spread about 1 cup of whipped topping on top. Unmold other layer, place on first layer and frost with remaining whipped topping. Refrigerate until ready to serve. Makes 12 servings.

Traditional Fruitcake

1 package date bar mix
⅔ cup hot water
3 eggs
¼ cup all-purpose flour
¾ teaspoon baking powder
2 tablespoons light molasses
1 teaspoon cinnamon
¼ teaspoon nutmeg
¼ teaspoon allspice
1 cup chopped nuts
1 cup raisins
1 cup red/green candied cherries

Heat oven to 325 degrees. Grease and flour a 9x5x3-inch loaf pan. Combine date bar mix and water until crumbly. Add eggs, flour, baking powder, molasses and spices. Fold in nuts, raisins and cherries; pour into pan. Bake 80 minutes or until toothpick comes out clean. Cool.

Pound Cake

2 sticks margarine or butter
½ cup shortening
3 cups sugar
5 eggs, beaten
3 cups all-purpose flour, sifted
½ teaspoon salt
6 ounces evaporated milk
2 teaspoons vanilla

Mix all ingredients and pour into a greased bundt pan. Bake at 325 degrees for 1 hour and 45 minutes. Cool on a rack before serving.

Christmas Jam Cake

2 cups sugar
1 cup butter
3 eggs
2 cups jam
1 teaspoon vanilla
1 teaspoon baking soda
1 cup buttermilk
1 teaspoon allspice
1 teaspoon nutmeg
1 teaspoon cloves
1 teaspoon cinnamon
3 cups self-rising flour
1½ cups nuts
1½ cups raisins
1 cup coconut
Icing

Cream sugar and butter. Add eggs and jam. Put baking soda and vanilla in buttermilk and mix seasonings in flour. Alternate milk and flour, mixing well. Add nuts, raisins and coconut. Pour in a greased bundt pan and bake at 300 degrees for 45 minutes.

Jam Cake Icing

2 cups sugar
1 cup butter
1½ cups milk
Chopped nuts

Combine all ingredients and cook until thickened. Add nuts and put pan in cold water. Beat until thick. Using a toothpick poke holes in cake and pour icing over top.

Meredith's Chocolate Pound Cake

2½ cups all-purpose flour
½ teaspoon salt
½ teaspoon baking soda
6 chocolate candy bars
2 sticks butter
2 cups sugar
4 eggs
1 cup buttermilk
2 teaspoons vanilla
1 cup chocolate sauce

Sift flour, salt and baking soda together. Melt chocolate candy bars and butter; add to sugar, eggs, buttermilk, vanilla and chocolate sauce. Add dry ingredients to chocolate mixture. Grease a bundt pan with butter and bake at 350 degrees for 1½ hours or until done. Drizzle top with melted chocolate and garnish with cherries.

Marilyn's Coconut Cake

White cake mix
8 ounces sour cream
¾ cup sugar
12 ounces frozen coconut, thawed

Bake two layer cakes according to package directions. Mix sour cream, sugar and 1¼ cups coconut. After cake has cooled, cover layers with icing and pat on remaining coconut. Let sit before cutting.

Pat's Praline Cheesecake

1½ pounds cream cheese
2 cups brown sugar
3 eggs
2 tablespoons self-rising flour
2 teaspoons vanilla
½ cup pecans
1 cup graham cracker crumbs
3 tablespoons sugar
3 tablespoons butter

Combine cream cheese and brown sugar in mixer; when thoroughly mixed add eggs, flour, vanilla and pecans. For crust, mix graham cracker crumbs, sugar and butter and put in a 10-inch spring form pan. Pour cream cheese mixture into crust and bake at 350 degrees for 35 minutes.

Miniature Cheesecakes

½ cup graham cracker crumbs
2 tablespoons butter or margarine, melted
8 ounces cream cheese, softened
¼ cup sugar
1 egg
½ teaspoon vanilla
10 ounces cherry preserves

Combine graham cracker crumbs and butter, mixing well. Line muffin pans with paper liners. Spoon 1 teaspoon graham cracker mixture into each liner; gently press into bottom. Beat cream cheese with mixer until light and fluffy; gradually add sugar and mix well. Add egg and vanilla; beat well. Spoon mixture into liners. Bake at 350 degrees for 10 minutes. Place cherry preserves in a saucepan; heat just until preserves melt. Spoon 1 teaspoon preserves over each cheesecake. Chill thoroughly. Makes 2 dozen.

Diane's Orange Bundt Cake

Yellow cake mix
½ cup margarine
½ cup orange juice
½ cup water
½ cup vegetable oil
1 box vanilla instant pudding
4 eggs
Glaze

Mix well all ingredients except glaze and pour into a greased bundt pan. Bake at 350 degrees for 30 minutes.

Orange Bundt Cake Glaze

½ cup orange juice
1 stick margarine
1 cup sugar

Mix all ingredients and boil for 3 minutes. Using a toothpick, poke holes in top of cake when removed from oven. Pour glaze over cake and let stand 20 minutes.

Cranberry-Pecan Upside-Down Cake

1½ cups cranberries
½ cup chopped pecans
½ cup butterscotch topping
⅓ cup margarine
⅔ cups sugar
1 egg
½ teaspoon vanilla
1 cup all-purpose flour
1½ teaspoons baking powder
½ teaspoon salt
½ cup milk

Arrange cranberries and pecans in bottom of a greased 8-inch square pan. Pour topping over. Cream margarine and sugar until light and fluffy. Blend in egg and vanilla. Combine dry ingredients; add to creamed mixture alternately with milk, mixing well after each addition. Pour batter over topping mixture. Bake at 350 degrees for 45 minutes, or until a toothpick inserted comes out clean. Immediately invert onto serving platter. Serve warm topped with whipped cream or ice cream.

Edna Trull
Nuts About Pecans

Buttermilk Pie

2 cups sugar
2 tablespoons flour
4 eggs
½ teaspoon vanilla
½ cup buttermilk
⅓ cup margarine

Mix sugar and flour; beat eggs and sugar-flour mixture until fluffy. Add vanilla, buttermilk and margarine. Mix well and put in an unbaked 9-inch pie shell. Bake at 350 degrees for 40 to 45 minutes.

No Crust Chocolate Pie

6 tablespoons cocoa
1 stick margarine
2 eggs
1 cup sugar
¼ cup self-rising flour
1 teaspoon vanilla

Melt cocoa and margarine. Beat together eggs, sugar, flour and vanilla. Let cocoa cool and add to the egg mixture, beating to combine; pour into a greased pie pan. Bake at 350 degrees for 25 to 30 minutes. Serve with ice cream or whipped topping.

Wonderful Pecan Cream Cheese Pie

6 ounces cream cheese, softened
½ cup sugar
4 eggs
2 teaspoons vanilla
¼ teaspoon salt
One unbaked 9-inch pastry shell
1¼ cups chopped pecans
¾ cup light or dark corn syrup
3 tablespoons sugar
3 tablespoons margarine or butter, melted

Beat cream cheese on medium speed until smooth. Add sugar, 1 of the eggs, 1 teaspoon vanilla and salt; beat until combined. Spread cream cheese mixture onto the bottom of the pastry. Sprinkle pecans over the cream cheese mixture. Whisk the remaining 3 eggs. Stir in the corn syrup, 3 tablespoons sugar, margarine or butter and the remaining 1 teaspoon vanilla. Place partially filled pastry on a baking sheet on oven rack. Slowly pour syrup mixture over pecans. Bake at 375 degrees for 20 minutes or more, until a knife inserted comes out clean. Cool pie on wire rack. Makes 8 servings.

Crème Brûlée

2 cups whipping cream
5 egg yolks
½ cup sugar
1 tablespoon vanilla extract
½ cup light brown sugar, firmly packed
Fresh raspberries or mint sprigs, for garnish

Combine first four ingredients, stirring with a wire whisk until sugar dissolves and mixture is smooth. Pour evenly into five buttered 5x1-inch round individual baking dishes; place dishes in a large roasting pan. Add hot water to pan to ½-inch depth. Bake at 275 degrees for 45 to 50 minutes or until almost set. Cool custards. Remove from pan; cover and chill at least 8 hours. Sprinkle about 1½ tablespoons brown sugar evenly over each custard; place custards in pan. Broil 5½ inches from heat, with door partially opened, until sugar melts. Let stand 5 minutes to allow sugar to harden. Garnish, if desired. Makes 5 servings.

Chilled Citrus Ambrosia

9 large oranges, peeled, seeded and sectioned
20 ounces pineapple chunks, drained
16 ounces fruit cocktail, drained
2 medium apples, unpeeled and coarsely chopped
2 cups sliced bananas
1 cup coconut
1 cup chopped pecans

Combine all ingredients, tossing well. Chill thoroughly. Makes 10 servings.

Dieter's Dream Brownies

1 box brownie mix
½ cup plain nonfat yogurt
Water, amount suggested on package

Grease bottom of 13x9x2-inch pan. Preheat oven to 350 degrees (325 degrees for a glass pan). Combine brownie mix, yogurt, and water. Mix well. Spread in pan. Bake 30 minutes or until done. Cool completely. Makes 24 brownies.

Candies

&

Cookies

Peppermint Balls

2 tablespoons cream cheese, at room temperature
1 teaspoon milk
½ cup powdered sugar
2 tablespoons finely crushed peppermint candies
1 drop red food coloring
1 cup butter
½ cup powdered sugar
2⅓ cups all-purpose flour
1 teaspoon vanilla
¼ cup powdered sugar
6 tablespoons finely crushed peppermint candies

Combine cream cheese and milk and add powdered sugar slowly. Stir in candy and food coloring, set aside for filling.

Cream butter and powdered sugar. Mix in vanilla, then add flour. Knead dough into balls, make a deep well in center of each ball with handle of wooden spoon. Fill with ¼ teaspoon of filling, shape a scant ¼ teaspoon of dough into a flat round, lay on top of filling; press gently to seal. Place on ungreased cookie sheet, bake at 350 degrees for 12 minutes. Roll warm cookies in combined powdered sugar and peppermint candy. Makes 4 dozen balls.

Snow Candy

1 pound white chocolate bark candy
1 pound salted nuts
2 cups crispy rice cereal

Melt candy in a double boiler. Add nuts and cereal. Mix well. Spoon onto waxed paper. Refrigerate until firm. Break into pieces; store in air tight container.

Divinity

2½ cups sugar
½ cup white corn syrup
¼ teaspoon salt
½ cup water
2 egg whites
1 teaspoon vanilla

In a saucepan, combine sugar, syrup, salt and water. Cook to hard ball stage. Stir only until sugar dissolves. While mixture is cooking, beat egg whites until stiff peaks form. When mixture reaches 260 degrees, pour egg whites in slowly, stirring constantly with mixer on high speed. Add vanilla when candy holds shape. Drop by teaspoon on waxed paper.

Buck Eye Candy

1 pound powdered sugar
One 8-ounce jar peanut butter
1½ sticks butter
½ bar paraffin
12 ounces chocolate chips

Cream powdered sugar, peanut butter and butter together and form into balls. Put on cookie sheet and chill. While chilling melt paraffin and chocolate chips. Using a toothpick dip balls in chocolate mix and place on waxed paper to dry.

Hard-Crack Candy

2 cups sugar
½ cup water
½ cup light corn syrup
½ teaspoon strawberry flavoring
10 drops red food coloring
1 tablespoon powdered sugar

Combine first 3 ingredients in a saucepan. Cook over medium heat, stirring occasionally, to hard crack stage or until candy thermometer reaches 300 degrees. Stir in strawberry flavoring and food coloring. Pour into a jellyroll pan dusted with powdered sugar; let cool. Break into pieces. Makes 1 pound.

Peanut Butter Fudge

4 cups sugar
1 stick butter
1 can evaporated milk
1 tablespoon vanilla
1½ cups peanut butter
1 pint marshmallow cream

Bring first 3 ingredients to a boil. Boil for 11 minutes. Mix remaining three ingredients. When mixture is finished boiling, pour over the remaining ingredients. Beat well and pour into a buttered 9x13-inch pan. Allow to cool and cut into pieces.

Everyone's Favorite Fudge

6 cups sugar
1½ cups butter
1 large can evaporated milk
2 packages chocolate chips
1 jar marshmallow cream
1 cup nuts

Combine sugar, butter and milk and cook in heavy pan until it begins to boil. Boil 10 minutes, stirring constantly. Remove from heat and add chips, marshmallow cream and nuts, making sure to mix well. Pour into a 9x13-inch buttered pan. When set cut into squares and store in an airtight container. Makes 6 pounds.

Chocolate Fudge

1 cup milk
1 teaspoon vanilla
4 cups sugar
1 cup butter
25 large marshmallows, cut in fourths or equivalent in miniatures or creme
12 ounces chocolate chips
12 ounces milk chocolate stars
2 ounces unsweetened chocolate
Pecans or walnuts, optional

Have all ingredients ready as you must work quickly.

Mix milk and vanilla in large saucepan. Add sugar and stir well, cooking over medium heat. Add butter and bring to a boil. Boil for two minutes, stirring constantly; remove from heat. Add marshmallows and stir until melted; add chocolate chips and stir, then stars, then unsweetened chocolate. Mix well and add nuts, if desired. Pour into buttered 13x9-inch pan. This will keep in the freezer if wrapped properly. Makes 3 pounds, 12 ounces.

Edna's Peanut Brittle

2 cups sugar
1 cup light corn syrup
1 cup water
2 cups unroasted peanuts
¼ teaspoon salt
1 teaspoon butter
1 teaspoon soda
1 teaspoon vanilla

Combine sugar, corn syrup and water. Cook to 236 degrees. Add peanuts and salt and cook to 295 degrees or hard crack stage. Remove and immediately add butter, soda and vanilla. It will foam up so you must stir constantly; pour quickly into a 9x13-inch buttered pan. Allow to harden.

Paula's Chocolate Brickle

Vegetable cooking spray
12 graham crackers
1 cup butter or margarine
1 cup sugar
12 ounces semi-sweet chocolate morsels
6 ounces almond brickle chips

Line a 15x10x1-inch pan with foil and coat with spray. Place graham crackers in a single layer to cover prepared pan and set aside. Combine butter and sugar in saucepan. Bring to a boil over medium heat, stirring constantly. Boil 1½ to 2 minutes, without stirring. Pour mixture over graham crackers. Bake at 350 degrees for 5 minutes. Remove from the oven and sprinkle with chocolate chips. Let stand until morsels are soft enough to spread. Spread smoothly over top. Sprinkle with brickle, press lightly. Cool and cut into 1½-inch squares. Makes 5 dozen squares.

Marilyn's Christmas Candy

1 pound powdered sugar
1 cup coconut
1 cup chopped pecans
1 teaspoon vanilla
1 cup graham cracker crumbs
½ cup crunchy peanut butter
1 cup butter, melted
½ bar paraffin
6 ounces semi-sweet chocolate chips

Thoroughly mix sugar, coconut, pecans, vanilla and graham cracker crumbs into the peanut butter. Pour melted butter over the mixture and blend well. Shape dough into balls. Melt paraffin and chocolate chips together over boiling water. Using a toothpick dip balls into the chocolate and place on waxed paper.

Bourbon Balls

3 cups vanilla wafers
1 cup pecans
1 cup powdered sugar
3 tablespoons light corn syrup
1½ tablespoons cocoa
½ cup bourbon

Grind wafers and nuts finely in food chopper. Mix with other ingredients thoroughly. Roll into balls the size of large cherries. Dust with powdered sugar. Makes 30 to 35 balls.

Florence Ross
Elizabeth Ross
Kentucky Keepsakes

Christmas Caramel Pecan Rolls

1¼ cups sifted powdered sugar
½ cup whipping cream
1 cup coarsely chopped pecans
2 loaves frozen sweet or white bread dough, thawed
3 tablespoons margarine or butter, melted
½ cup packed brown sugar
1 tablespoon ground cinnamon

Topping: In a small mixing bowl stir together powdered sugar and whipping cream. Divide evenly between two 9x1½-inch round baking pans. Sprinkle pecans evenly over sugar mixture. Roll each loaf of dough into a 12x8-inch rectangle on a lightly floured surface. Brush with melted margarine or butter.

In a small mixing bowl stir together brown sugar and cinnamon; sprinkle over dough. Roll up rectangles, jelly-roll style, starting from a long side. Pinch to seal. Cut each into 10 to 12 slices. Place rolls, cut side down on top of pecan mixture. Cover with a warm towel. Let rise in a warm place until nearly double, about 30 minutes. Bake rolls, uncovered, at 375 degrees until golden. If necessary, cover rolls with foil the last 10 minutes to prevent over-browning. Cool in pans 5 minutes on a wire rack. Invert onto serving platter. Serve warm. Makes 20 to 24 rolls.

Goody Goody Gumdrop Cookie Mix

1 ½ cups gumdrops
1 cup granulated sugar
4 cups all-purpose flour
1 cup packed brown sugar
2 teaspoons baking powder
1 ½ cups shortening
1 egg
1 teaspoon vanilla

Chop gumdrops into small pieces. Toss with ¼ cup sugar, until well coated. Set aside. Stir the flour, remaining sugar, brown sugar and baking powder together in a large mixing bowl. Cut in the shortening until the mixture resembles fine crumbs. Stir together the gumdrops, cookie mix, egg and vanilla. Shape dough into 1½-inch balls. Place balls 2 inches apart on an ungreased cookie sheet. Flatten slightly with the bottom of a glass dipped in sugar. Bake at 375 degrees for 8 to 10 minutes or until bottoms are lightly browned. Remove and cool completely on wire racks. Makes about 48 cookies.

Ginger Cookies

1 stick butter, softened
½ cup packed dark brown sugar
1 tablespoon fresh ginger, peeled and finely minced
½ teaspoon vanilla
1 tablespoon ground ginger
1¼ cups all-purpose flour
¼ teaspoon baking soda
Pinch of salt
3 to 4 pieces crystallized ginger, cut into small pieces

Cream the butter, sugar and fresh ginger together until smooth. Add vanilla. Mix ginger, flour, baking soda and salt together. Add dry ingredients to butter mixture, just to combine. Form dough into log about 2 inches square, wrap in plastic wrap and chill until firm or about 1 hour. Preheat oven to 350 degrees. Slice log into ¼-inch slices, top each with a sliver of crystallized ginger pressed into the center. Bake until lightly golden or 8 to 10 minutes. Remove to a rack to cool completely. Makes 30 cookies.

M & M and Chocolate Chews

1¼ cups butter
2 eggs
2 cups sugar
2 teaspoons vanilla
2 cups all-purpose flour
1 teaspoon baking soda
1 cup chocolate chips
¼ cup cocoa
½ teaspoon salt
1 cup M&M's

Cream butter, eggs, sugar and vanilla well. In a separate bowl, mix together flour, baking soda, chips, cocoa and salt. Mix wet mixture and dry mixture together. Spread ½ mixture into a lightly greased 9x13-inch pan. Top with M&M's and then remaining dough. Bake at 375 degrees for 25 to 30 minutes.

Peanut Clusters

2 pounds almond bark
12 ounces chocolate chips
1 pound peanuts

Melt almond bark in double boiler; add chips. Mix until smooth and stir in peanuts. Drop by teaspoonfuls onto waxed paper. Cool.

Santa's Favorite Molasses Cookies

¾ cup shortening
¼ cup molasses
1 cup sugar
1 egg
2 cups all-purpose flour
2 teaspoons baking soda
½ teaspoon salt
½ teaspoon cloves
½ teaspoon ginger
1 teaspoon cinnamon

Melt shortening in a sauce pan over low heat. Remove from heat and allow to cool. Add molasses, sugar and egg. Beat well. Sift flour, soda, salt and spices. Add flour mixture to molasses mixture and mix well. Wrap in plastic and chill overnight. Form into 1-inch balls and roll each in granulated sugar. Place on a lightly greased cookie sheet and bake for 8 to 10 minutes at 350 degrees. Cool before serving.

Santa's Elves Sugar Cookies

1 cup shortening
1 cup sugar
2 eggs
1 teaspoon vanilla
2¾ cups sifted all-purpose flour
¾ teaspoon salt
½ teaspoon baking powder
½ teaspoon baking soda

Cream shortening and sugar. Beat in eggs and vanilla. Sift dry ingredients together and blend into mixture. Chill dough for 3 hours. Roll out into balls on lightly floured board. Flatten with bottom of a glass dipped in sugar. Bake on ungreased cookie sheets at 375 degrees for 8 to 10 minutes or until done. Cool on wire rack.

Chocolate Snowball Cookies

¼ cup butter or margarine, softened
½ cup sugar
1 egg
1 square unsweetened chocolate, melted
1 teaspoon vanilla
1½ cups all-purpose flour
½ teaspoon baking powder
¼ teaspoon salt
Snow Glaze

Cream butter; gradually add sugar, beating until light and fluffy. Add next 3 ingredients and beat well. Combine flour, baking powder and salt; gradually add to creamed mixture, beating until smooth. Chill dough 1 to 2 hours. Shape dough into 1-inch balls. Place on greased cookie sheet. Bake at 350 degrees for 12 minutes. Cool and dip into Snow Glaze. Makes 3 dozen.

Snow Glaze

1 cup sifted powdered sugar
1 tablespoon and 2 teaspoons milk
½ teaspoon vanilla

Combine all ingredients and beat until smooth.

Holiday Bears

½ cup peanut butter
¼ cup margarine or butter
¼ cup shortening
⅔ cup granulated sugar
⅓ cup packed brown sugar
¾ teaspoon baking soda
1 egg
½ teaspoon vanilla
1 cup all-purpose flour
½ cup finely crushed graham crackers
Miniature semi-sweet chocolate pieces
Frosting

Beat peanut butter, margarine or butter and shortening with mixer for 30 seconds. Add granulated sugar, brown sugar, baking soda, egg and vanilla; beat until combined. Beat in as much of the flour and cracker crumbs as you can with the mixer on medium speed, scraping the sides of the bowl occasionally. Stir in any remaining flour and crumbs with a wooden spoon. For each bear cookie, shape some of dough into one 1¼-inch ball (for body), one ¾-inch ball (for head), three balls slightly smaller than ¼-inch (for nose and ears), two 1½x½-inch logs (for arms)and two 1¼x¾-inch logs (for legs).

Flatten the ball for body to 1¾-inch round on an ungreased cookie sheet. Attach the ball for the head; flatten to 1¼-inch round. Attach the small balls to the head for nose and ears. Attach the logs for arms and legs. Decorate bears before baking by pressing in chocolate pieces, point side up, for eyes. For paws, press chocolate pieces point side down, onto ends of arms and legs. Bake at 325 degrees for 15 to 18 minutes or until edges are lightly browned. Cool on cookie sheet 2 to 3 minutes. Remove cookies and cool on a wire rack. Add colorful frosting trims. Makes about 20 bears.

Mom's No Bake Oatmeal Cookies

1 stick butter
½ cup milk
2 cups sugar
⅓ cup cocoa
½ cup peanut butter
1 teaspoon vanilla
1 teaspoon salt
3 cups oats

Mix first four ingredients and boil 1 minute. Remove from heat and immediately add remaining ingredients. Stir until folds into shape. Drop by spoon onto waxed paper. Let cool before serving.

Gift Giving Goodies

Christmas Gift Preserves

8 kiwi fruits
2 large ripe pears
4 cups sugar
3 ounces liquid fruit pectin
½ teaspoon finely shredded lime or lemon peel
2 tablespoons lime or lemon juice

Peel and chop kiwi fruit. Peel, core and chop pears. Stir together the fruits. Stir in the sugar. Let stand 10 minutes. Combine the pectin, lime or lemon peel and lime or lemon juice. Add to the fruit mixture. Stir for 3 minutes. Ladle the mixture into half-pint freezer jars, leaving ½-inch headspace. Seal and label. Let stand at room temperature several hours or until set. Makes about 6 half-pint gifts.

Toasty Party Mix

⅓ cup margarine or butter
1 tablespoon soy sauce
¾ teaspoon chili powder
⅛ teaspoon garlic powder
⅛ teaspoon ground red pepper
3 cups bite-size corn-and-rice square cereal
3 ounces chow mein noodles
1 cup peanuts
1 cup shelled, raw pumpkin seeds

Mix margarine or butter, soy sauce, chili powder, garlic powder and red pepper in a small saucepan. Cook and stir until margarine melts. Mix cereal, chow mein noodles, peanuts and pumpkin seeds in a roasting pan. Drizzle margarine mixture over noodle mixture; toss to coat. Bake at 300 degrees for 30 minutes, stirring every 10 minutes. Spread on foil to cool. Store in an airtight container. Makes 12 to 15 servings.

Gift Giving Raspberry Vinegar

1½ cups fresh or 6 ounces frozen red raspberries
2 cups white vinegar
1 cup dry white wine

In a saucepan bring all ingredients to a boil. Boil gently, uncovered, for 3 minutes. Remove from heat and cool slightly. Pour the mixture into a hot 1-quart jar. Cover loosely with a lid (do not use metal). Let the jar stand until mixture cools completely. Then cover the jar tightly with the non-metal lid. Let vinegar stand in a cool, dark place for 1 week.

After 1 week, line a colander with cheesecloth or a cup-shaped coffee filter. Pour the vinegar through the colander and let in drain into a bowl. Transfer the strained vinegar to a clean 1½-pint bottle or jar. Makes about 3 cups.

Holiday Salsa

28 ounces tomatoes, drained, seeded and finely chopped
3 tablespoons finely chopped onion
3 tablespoons finely chopped green pepper
3 tablespoons finely chopped jalapeño pepper
1 tablespoon snipped fresh cilantro or 1 teaspoon dried cilantro, crushed
1 tablespoon red wine vinegar
2 cloves garlic, minced
¼ teaspoon salt
Several dashes of hot pepper sauce
Dash of pepper

Combine the tomatoes, onion, green pepper, jalapeño pepper, cilantro, vinegar, garlic, salt, hot pepper sauce and pepper. Transfer salsa to a container. Seal and refrigerate for 3 to 8 hours, stirring occasionally. Makes about 1½ cups sauce.

Marmalade for your Hostess

2 large oranges
2 large lemons
1 cup unsweetened pineapple juice
20 ounces crushed pineapple, undrained
1¾ ounces powdered fruit pectin
5 cups sugar

Score citrus peel into four lengthwise sections. Remove peel with a vegetable peeler. Cut into very thin strips. Combine peels and pineapple juice. Cover and simmer 20 minutes; do not drain. Cut white membrane off fruit. Section fruit over bowl to catch juices. Discard seeds. Add fruits and juices to peel mixture. Simmer, uncovered, 10 minutes more. Add pineapple. Transfer fruit mixture to an 8-quart Dutch oven; stir in pectin. Bring to a full rolling boil, stirring constantly. Stir in sugar; return to full rolling boil. Boil hard 1 minute, stirring constantly. Remove from heat; quickly skim off foam. Ladle at once into hot sterilized half-pint jars, leaving ¼-inch headspace. Wipe rims; adjust lids. Process in boiling-water bath 15 minutes (start timing when water boils). Makes 7 half-pints.

Cranberry Relish

2 cups sugar
¾ cup orange juice
4 cups cranberries, fresh or frozen
2 teaspoons grated orange rind

Combine sugar and orange juice in a saucepan, stirring well; add cranberries and orange rind. Bring to a boil over medium heat, stirring often. Reduce heat and simmer 5 minutes or until cranberry skins pops and mixture thickens. Makes 4 cups.

Soy Sauce Marinade

½ cup soy sauce
½ cup water
2 tablespoons lemon juice
1 tablespoon brown sugar
2 tablespoons vegetable oil
¼ teaspoon hot sauce
1 clove garlic, crushed
¼ teaspoon freshly ground pepper

Combine all ingredients. Use for marinade on beef, pork or chicken.

Southwestern Marinade

1 tablespoon cumin seeds
1 teaspoon coriander seeds
8 dried chilies, stemmed and seeded
1 tablespoon brown sugar
1 teaspoon ground cinnamon
½ teaspoon garlic powder
½ teaspoon salt
¼ teaspoon black pepper
¼ teaspoon ground red pepper

Cook cumin and coriander seeds in a small skillet over low heat, stirring constantly for 3 minutes. Combine seeds, chilies and remaining ingredients with a electric blender until mixture resembles coarse powder. Store in an airtight container. Makes ⅔ cup.

Curried Almond Treat

3 cups blanched whole almonds
1 tablespoon butter or margarine, melted
2 teaspoons seasoned salt
¾ teaspoon curry powder

Place almonds in a shallow roasting pan; brush butter over nuts and stir well. Roast almonds at 350 degrees for 20 minutes or until golden brown. Combine salt and curry powder; sprinkle over almonds and stir until well coated. Bake an additional 10 minutes. Drain on paper towels and let cool. Makes about 3 cups.

Sugar and Spice and Everything Nice Pecans

¾ cup sugar
1 egg white
2½ tablespoons water
1 teaspoon ground cinnamon
½ teaspoon salt
¼ teaspoon allspice
¼ teaspoon ground cloves
¼ teaspoon ground nutmeg
8 cups pecan halves

Combine first 8 ingredients and mix well. Add pecans and stir until evenly coated. Spread pecans in a greased jellyroll pan. Bake at 275 degrees for 50 to 55 minutes. Remove to waxed paper and let cool. Makes 9 cups.

Apricot Butter

2 cups firmly packed dried apricots
4 cups water
2 cups sugar

Combine apricots and water; let stand 8 hours. Cook apricots, uncovered, 8 to 10 minutes. Press apricots through a coarse sieve, discarding pulp. Bring to a boil; add sugar and simmer 40 to 45 minutes, stirring frequently. Quickly spoon into hot sterilized jars with metal lids. Process in boiling water bath for 10 minutes. Makes 4 half-pints.

Great Gift Granola

3 cups regular oats
1 cup unsalted sunflower kernels
1 cup chopped pecans
½ cup wheat germ
½ cup sesame seeds
½ cup honey
¼ cup vegetable oil
¼ cup vanilla extract
1 cup raisins

Combine first 5 ingredients; mix well and set aside. Combine honey and oil and cook over medium heat, stirring until mixture is thoroughly heated. Remove from heat; stir in vanilla, mixing well. Pour over oats mixture and stir until evenly coated. Spread mixture into a lightly greased jellyroll pan. Bake at 250 degrees for 50 minutes, stirring every 10 minutes; cool. Add raisins and mix well. Store in an airtight container. Makes 8 cups.

Zesty Spinach Pesto

4 cups firmly packed fresh or well-drained frozen spinach
½ cup dried basil
1 cup grated Parmesan cheese
½ cup chopped walnuts
1 cup olive oil
8 cloves garlic
½ teaspoon salt
¼ teaspoon pepper

Blend all ingredients except spinach on high speed about 1 minute, stopping occasionally to scrape sides. Add spinach, 1 cup at a time, blending until smooth. Can be stored in refrigerator or freezer. Makes 3 cups.

Chocolate Sauce

⅓ cup sugar
¼ cup cocoa
⅓ cup water
3 tablespoons light corn syrup
1 teaspoon vanilla
½ teaspoon chocolate extract

Combine sugar, cocoa, water and corn syrup and cook over medium heat until mixture boils, stirring constantly. Boil 2 minutes, stirring constantly, until smooth and glossy. Remove from heat; stir in vanilla and chocolate extract. Serve warm or cool. Makes ⅔ cup.

Caramel Corn

3 quarts popped popcorn
1 cup brown sugar, packed
½ cup butter, softened
¼ cup light corn syrup
½ teaspoon salt
½ teaspoon vanilla
½ teaspoon baking soda
Brown paper bag

Pour popcorn into bag, set aside. In a microwave safe bowl, mix brown sugar, butter, corn syrup and salt. Microwave on high for 2 minutes. Add vanilla and soda. Quickly pour over popcorn. Fold top down on bag and shake well. Microwave 1½ minutes. Shake well and microwave 1½ minutes more. Pour onto 2 cookie sheets. Let cool and break into pieces. Store in an airtight container.

Delightful Almond-Coffee Toffee

6 ounces unsalted blanched almonds, coarsely chopped
1 cup butter
1½ cups sugar
¼ cup brewed coffee
1 tablespoon light corn syrup
½ cup dark roast coffee beans, coarsely chopped
24 ounces semi-sweet chocolate, grated

Preheat oven to 350 degrees. Line a 9x13-inch baking sheet with foil; butter the foil. Spread the almonds evenly over a second baking sheet and toast them until lightly browned, 10 to 12 minutes. Remove from the oven. Stir the butter, sugar, coffee and syrup in a saucepan over medium heat until butter melts and sugar dissolves. Bring to a boil and simmer without stirring until the mixture reaches 300 degrees. Quickly stir in the almond an coffee beans. Pour immediately onto the buttered baking sheet and cool completely. Melt the chocolate gently into top of a double boiler or in microwave. Spread half of chocolate evenly over toffee. When chocolate has set, invert the sheet of toffee onto waxed paper and remove the liner. Spread the remaining chocolate over inverted toffee. When chocolate has set, break toffee into pieces. Store in an airtight container.

December Events
in
Kentucky

This list serves as a sampling of events in Kentucky during the Christmas season. Call your local Chamber of Commerce or Tourist Commission for a complete list. For events listed call ahead for correct times and dates.

Babes in Toyland, Paramount Arts Center, Ashland. 606-324-3175 or 606-329-0417
Brass Band of the Tri-State Christmas Concert, Paramount Arts Center, Ashland. 606-324-3175
Christmas Tour of Homes, Ashland. 606-329-1826
Holiday Fashion Show, Ashland. 606-324-1100
Kentucky Quilts Exhibit, Kentucky Highland Museum, Ashland. 606-329-8888
Kid's Christmas Workshop, Kentucky Highland Museum, Ashland. 606-329-8888
Lunch with Santa, Kentucky Highland Museum, Ashland. 606-329-8888
New Year's Eve on the Plaza, Ashland. 800-377-6249
The Nutcracker, Paramount Arts Center, Ashland. 606-324-3175
Scottish Walk, Kentucky Highland Museum, Ashland. 606-329-8888
Sounds of the Season, Ashland Town Center, Ashland. 606-324-1100
Winter Wonderland of Lights, Ashland. 800-377-6249
Christmas Country Dance School, Berea. 606-986-9341
Christmas in Berea, Berea. 606-986-2540
Christmas Parade, Bowling Green. 502-782-0037
Lighting of Fountain Square Park, Bowling Green. 502-782-0037
Christmas Island, General Burnside State Park, Burnside. 800-642-6287
Christmas Parade, Cadiz. 502-552-3892
Christmas Sparkles on Main Street, Cadiz. 502-522-3892
The Holiday House, Cadiz. 502-522-3892
Central City Christmas Celebration, Central City. 502-926-1100
Central City Wreath Lighting Ceremony, Central City. 502-754-2360
Kentucky's Largest Small Town Christmas Parade, Central City. 502-854-2306 or 502-754-9603
Lunch with St. Nicholas, MainStrasse Village, Covington. 606-491-0458
Winterlights at MainStrasse Village, Covington. 606-491-0458
Christmas Remembered at Constitution Square, Danville. 606-239-7089
Christmas on the Dry Ridge, Dry Ridge. 800-382-7117
Christmas in the Park, Freeman Lake Park, Elizabethtown. 800-437-0092
Old Fashion Christmas in the City, Brown Pusey House, Elizabethtown. 800-438-0092
Christmas at Kincaid Lake, Falmouth. 606-654-3531
Frankfort Arts and Crafts Bazaar, Frankfort. 502-227-9920
Frankfort Yuletide Festival and Madrigal, Frankfort. 502-227-7430
Christmas Parade, Georgetown. 502863-2547
Christmas in the Country, Glendale. 800-437-0092
Christmas Parade, Greenville. 502-338-5422
Holiday at Greenbo Lake Resort State Park, Greenup. 606-473-9881
New Year's Eve Dance, Greenbo Lake State Park, Greenup. 606-473-9881
Christmas at the Center, Duncan Cultural Center, Greenville. 502-926-1100
Christmas Parade, Greenville. 502-338-3966 or 502-338-5422
Hanson Christmas Craft Show, Hanson. 502-322-8375
Christmas in the Park, Kenlake State Park, Hardin. 800-467-7145

Shaker Order of Christmas, Harrodsburg. 606-734-5411
Shaker Village Simple Gifts of Christmas, Harrodsburg. 606-734-5411
Christmas Parade, Hawesville. 502-926-1100
Christmas in the Park, Central Park, Henderson. 502-827-0016
Henderson's "Homes" for the Holiday Home Tour, Henderson. 502-826-4410
Holiday Hop, Henderson Fine Arts Center, Henderson. 502-926-1100
Rudy Rowland Christmas Tree Lighting, Henderson. 502-827-9881
Shrine Christmas Parade, Henderson. 502-827-9759
Hodgenville Christmas in the Park, Hodgenville. 502-358-3137
Christmas Parade, Hopkinsville. 502-887-4290
Hopkinsville Christmas Crafts Festival, Hopkinsville. 502-271-2989
Hopkinsville Heritage Crafts, Hopkinsville. 502-887-4270
Light Up LaGrange, LaGrange. 502-222-5072
Lebanon Junction Christmas in the City, Lebanon Junction. 502-833-2296
Leitchfield Hometown Christmas, Leitchfield. 502-259-5587
Christmas Parade, Lewisport. 502-926-1100
A Christmas Carol, Children's Theatre, Kentucky Horse Center, Lexington. 606-293-1853
Christmas Parade, Lewisport. 502-926-1100
Candlelight Tour at Waveland, Lexington. 502-564-4940
Christmas Creations Craft Show, Heritage Hall, Lexington. 606-233-4567
Christmas Parade, Lexington. 606-231-7335
Southern Lights Holiday Festival, Kentucky Horse Park, Lexington. 606-255-5727
Christmas Parade, Livermore. 502-926-1100
Christmas on Main, London. 606-864-4789
A Christmas Carol, Actors Theatre of Louisville. 502-581-1205
Gershwin on Ice, Palace Theatre, Louisville. 502-583-4555
The Gift of the Magi, Actors Theatre of Louisville, Louisville. 502-584-1205
Holidazzle, Kentucky Art and Craft Gallery, Louisville. 502-589-0102
Kentucky Derby Festival Children's Holiday Parade, Louisville. 502-584-3378
Louisville Ballet: *The Nutcracker*, Kentucky Center for the Arts, Louisville. 800-775-7777
Louisville Christmas Show, Commonwealth Convention Center, Louisville. 812-265-6100
The Louisville Pops, Palace Theatre, Louisville. 502-587-8687
Old Louisville Holiday House Tour, Louisville. 502-635-5244
Silver Bells, Derby Dinner Playhouse, Louisville. 812-288-8281
Sixth Annual Light Up the River, Ohio River, Louisville. 800-289-7245
A Merry Christmas with Brass, Fine Arts Center, Madisonville. 502-926-1100
Festival of Lights, Madisonville. 502-821-4963
Holiday Delights, City Park, Madisonville. 502-821-4963
Lighted Christmas Parade, Madisonville. 502-821-4963
Christmas Parade, Middlesboro. 606-248-1075
Christmas Home Tour in Mt. Washington, Mt. Washington. 800-526-2068

Light Up Mt. Washington, Mt. Washington. 502-538-3022
Christmas Parade, Murray. 800-651-1603
Ham Breakfast, Murray. 800-651-1603
Frontier Christmas at Old Washington, Old Washington. 606-759-7411
Candlelight Home and Light Tour, Owensboro. 502-281-4653
Christmas Parade, Owensboro. 502-683-2060
Holiday Homecoming Crafts Show, Executive Inn, Owensboro. 502-926-3661
Holiday in the Park, Legion Park, Owensboro. 502-687-8700
Owensboro First Night, Owensboro. 502-687-8700
Owensboro Symphony Christmas Pops Concert, River Park Center, Owensboro. 502-687-2787
Candlelight Christmas Trail, Paducah. 800-723-8224
Candlelight Tours of Historic Homes, Paducah. 800-723-8224
Christmas Parade, Paducah. 800-723-8224
The Downtown Antique Association Dickens Christmas, Paducah. 800-723-8224
Festival of Lights, Paducah. 800-723-8224
Horse-drawn Carriage Rides, Paducah. 800-723-8224
Jinglebell Run/Rudolph Romp, Paducah. 800-723-8224
Tree Lighting Ceremonies, Paducah. 800-723-8224
Trudy and the Minstrel, Market House Theatre, Paducah. 502-444-6828
Whitehaven Christmas Open House, Paducah. 502-554-2077
Appalachian Christmas Bazaar, Pikeville. 606-432-9326
Pikeville Hometown Christmas, Pikeville. 800-844-7453
Christmas Candlelight Tour, Adsmore Museum, Princeton. 502-365-3114
Christmas Parade, Princeton. 502-365-5393
Victorian Christmas, Adsmore Museum, Princeton. 502-365-3114
Christmas Parade, Providence. 502-667-2251
Christmas in the Valley, Renfro Valley. 800-765-7464
Richmond Celebration of Christmas, Richmond. 800-866-3705
Christmas Parade, Sacramento. 502-926-1100
Christmas Parade, Sebree. 502-926-1100
Christmas in Shepherdsville Square, Shepherdsville. 502-241-5100
Christmas Parade, Slaughters. 502-884-3275
Christmas Parade, Somerset. 606-679-7323
Christmas at Shakertown in South Union, South Union. 800-811-8379
Spencer County Farm Toy Show, Spencer County. 502-477-3255
Audubon Christmas Bird Count, Versailles. 606-873-5711
Christmas Parade, Versailles. 606-873-6326
Dickens of a Christmas, Vine Grove. 502-877-2121
Christmas on the Hill at West Point, West Point. 502-922-4560

INDEX

Soups and Salads

Merry Christmas from Kentucky

Mail to:
McClanahan Publishing House, Inc.
P. O. Box 100
Kuttawa, KY 42055

For Orders call TOLL FREE
1-800-544-6959
Visa & MasterCard accepted

Please send me _____ copies of

Merry Christmas from Kentucky   @ 19.95 $ each _____
                    Postage & handling   _____3.50___
Kentucky residents add 6% sales tax   @ 1.20   _____

                    Total enclosed   _____

Make check payable to McClanahan Publishing House

Ship to:
NAME _____

ADDRESS _____

CITY _____ STATE _____ ZIP _____

PLEASE COPY